C000109247

Where Did

Where Did Christianity Come From?

Justin Taylor, S.M.

A Michael Glazier Book
THE LITURGICAL PRESS
Collegeville, Minnesota

www.litpress.org

A Michael Glazier Book published by The Liturgical Press.

Cover design by David Manahan, O.S.B. Cover photo: view of the Negev Desert from Masada, Israel. FLAT EARTH PHOTOS.

1   2   3   4   5   6   7   8   9

Library of Congress Cataloging-in-Publication Data

Taylor, Justin, 1943–
        Where did Christianity come from? / Justin Taylor.
            p. cm.
        Includes bibliographical references and index.
        ISBN 0-8146-5102-X (alk. paper)
        1. Church history—Primitive and early church, ca. 30–600.
    2. Christianity—Origin. I. Title.

BR165.T32 2001
270.1—dc21   00-058904

For Allan and Diana Cockburn,
friends indeed

Contents

Acknowledgments   xi

Abbreviations   xiii

Introduction   1

CHAPTER ONE: STARTING POINTS   13

I. The Sources   13

    1. The New Testament   14
        a. New Testament and Kerygma   14
        b. The Acts of the Apostles   17
    2. Qumran Documents and Rabbinic Texts   19
        a. The Qumran Documents   19
        b. The Rabbinic Texts   20
    3. Philo and Josephus   21
        a. Philo of Alexandria   21
        b. Flavius Josephus   22
    4. Conclusions   24

II. Two Intriguing Episodes   26

    1. Peter and Cornelius (Acts 10:1-48)   26
    2. The Night at Troas (Acts 20:7-12)   29

CHAPTER TWO: BAPTISM AND EUCHARIST   34

I. Baptism   35

    1. John's Baptism   36

2. John, Jesus, and Their Disciples   40
3. The Baptism of Jesus and Christian Baptism   41

II. The Last Supper   44

1. The Problem of Chronology   44
2. Last Supper and Passover   46
3. Looking for a Meaning   48

III. Conclusions   55

CHAPTER THREE: JEWISH GALILEE   57

I. Galilee Until Herod   59

1. After the Exile   59
2. Around Herod the Great   61

II. Hillel and Galilee   64

1. A Distant Enthronement   64
2. An Essential Question About Passover   67

III. The Galilee That Jesus Knew   70

IV. Before and After the Downfall of Jerusalem   74

1. Josephus and Galilee   74
2. The Academy of Yavneh   75
3. Migration into Galilee after 135   78

V. From Fraternities to Schools   80

1. The Ideal of the Fraternity *(ḥabura)*   80
2. Proselyte Baptism   82

VI. Conclusions   85

CHAPTER FOUR: THE GENTILE MISSION   87

I. Jews and Gentiles   87

1. Jewish Proselytism?   87
2. Reformers and Rebels   90
   a. Pharisee Reformers   90
   b. Militant Activists   91
3. *Christiani* at Rome, Alexandria, Antioch   93

II. Ephesus and Corinth   101

    1. Apollos and Correct Teaching   102
    2. Paul, from Corinth to Ephesus   106
    3. The Disciples at Ephesus   108

III. The Beginnings of the Mission   111

    1. The Road to Damascus   112
    2. Events in Jerusalem   114
    3. Ascension and Pentecost   116

CHAPTER FIVE: JAMES, PAUL, AND PETER   118

I. James at Jerusalem   119

    1. The Jerusalem Decrees (Acts 15)   119
    2. Precepts for the Children of Noah   121

II. The Heritage of James   124

    1. The Jewish Bishops of Jerusalem   124
    2. The Nazoreans   125
    3. James's Eclipse and Return to Favor   128

III. Tannaites and Nazoreans   129

    1. Traces of Polemics   130
    2. The Danger of Christianity   131

IV. The Formation of the New Testament   133

    1. The Nazoreans and the Gospels   135
    2. Luke–Acts   137
    3. Toward a Canon   138
    4. Final Remarks   140

CHAPTER SIX: THE COVENANT   141

I. Passover   142

    1. The Paschal Lamb   142
    2. Passover and Easter   143

II. Pentecost and the Covenant   145

III. Admission and Exclusion   148

1. Initiation in the Name of the Trinity   149
2. Table Fellowship and Penalties   151

IV. Why *Christiani?*   152

1. Christians, Anointings   153
2. The Sign of the Cross   157
3. Conclusions   160

CHAPTER SEVEN: AND JESUS?   162

1. "A prophet powerful in words and in deeds"   163
2. "We were hoping . . ."   165
3. "Our leaders gave him up"   166
4. ". . . who said that he is living"   167

Conclusion   169

For Further Reading   172

Appendix: The "Slavonic" Josephus   174

Glossary of Terms and Names   177

Index of Scriptural References   180

Index of Non-Scriptural References   186

Acknowledgments

Étienne Nodet, O.P., encouraged me to produce this further fruit of our common labors and drew my attention to the "Slavonic" version of Josephus's Jewish War. My thanks are due also to Jerome Murphy O'Connor, O.P., and to Michael Patella, O.S.B., who read the manuscript and proposed a number of corrections and improvements.

Abbreviations

1 QH . . .   Documents from the Qumran caves; the most frequently
             cited are: 1 QH *(Hodayot/Thanksgiving Hymns);* 1 QM
             (War Scroll); 1 QS *(Rule of the Community/Manual of
             Discipline);* 1 QSa *(Rule of the Congregation/Messianic
             Rule);* 4 QMMT *(Miqsat ma'aśeh ha-Torah);* 4 QFl
             (Florilegium); 11 QT *(Temple Scroll);* CD *(Damascus
             Document).* There are English translations in: Flo-
             rentino García-Martínez, *The Dead Sea Scrolls Trans-
             lated: The Qumran Texts in English,* trans. Wilfred G. E.
             Watson from the Spanish edition, 1992 (Leiden–New
             York–Cologne–Grand Rapids, Mich.: E. J. Brill–
             Wm. B. Eerdmans, 2nd ed. with corrections and addi-
             tions, 1996); Geza Vermes, *The Complete Dead Sea
             Scrolls in English* (New York: Allen Lane–The Penguin
             Press, 1997).

Ab   Tractate *'Abot,* of the order *Neziqin* of the *Mishnah.*
AbZ   Tractate *'Aboda Zara,* of the order *Neziqin* of the *Mish-
             nah.*
Ant.   Flavius Josephus, *Jewish Antiquities.* Greek text and
             English translation by H. St. John Thackeray, Ralf Mar-
             cus, Allan Wikgren, and Louis H. Feldman, in Loeb
             Classical Library (London-Cambridge, Mass.: William
             Heinemann–Harvard University Press, vols. IV–IX). The
             classic English version by William Whiston continues to
             be republished.
AT   Alexandrian Text.
B . . .   (e.g. *BYoma* 11b) *Babylonian Talmud (Babli),* tractate
             (including the "minor tractates" without corresponding

	mishnah), usual pagination. There is an English translation in: I. Epstein, ed. *The Babylonian Talmud* (London: Soncino).
BabaB	Tractate *Baba Batra,* of the order *Neziqin* of the *Mishnah.*
Ber	Tractate *Berakhot,* of the order *Zeraʿim* of the *Mishnah.*
CD	*The Damascus Document* (see the first entry).
Clement . . .	For English translations of early Christian writers before the Council of Nicea (325 A.D.), see the series *The Ante-Nicene Fathers* (Edinburgh–Grand Rapids, Mich.: T. & T. Clark–Wm. B. Eerdmans).
Dem	Tractate *Demaʾi,* of the order *Zeraʿim* of the *Mishnah.*
Did.	*Didache* or *Teaching of the Twelve Apostles.* There is an English translation (also of other early texts) in: J. B. Lightfoot and J. R. Harmer, *The Apostolic Fathers,* 2nd ed. rev. and ed. by M. W. Holmes (Leicester: Apollos, 1990).
Eusebius . . .	For English translations of early Christian writers after the Council of Nicea (325 A.D.), see the series The Nicene and Post-Nicene Fathers (Edinburgh–Grand Rapids, Mich.: T. & T. Clark–Wm. B. Eerdmans).
Gk	Greek.
Ḥag	Tractate *Ḥagiga,* of the order *Moʿed* of the *Mishnah.*
Heb.	Hebrew.
Jub(ilees)	*The Book of Jubilees.* There are English translations in R. H. Charles, ed., *The Apocrypha and Pseudepigrapha of the Old Testament in English,* vol. 2 (Oxford: Clarendon, 1913); James H. Charlesworth, ed., *The Old Testament Pseudepigrapha,* vol. 2 (Garden City, N.Y.: Doubleday, 1985).
J.W.	Flavius Josephus, *The Jewish War.* Greek text and English translation by H. St. J. Thackeray, in Loeb Classical Library, vols. II–III (London–Cambridge, Mass.: William Heinemann–Harvard University Press). The classic English version by William Whiston continues to be republished.
Ker	Tractate *Keritut* (or: *Karetot*), of the order *Qodashim* of the *Mishnah.*
Life	Flavius Josephus, *The Life.* Greek text and English translation by H. St. J. Thackeray, in Loeb Classical Library, vol. I (London–Cambridge, Mass.: William Heinemann–Harvard University Press).

LXX	The Septuagint (Greek translation of the Old Testament begun at Alexandria from about 250 B.C.).
M . . .	(e.g., *MPea* 3:2) *Mishnah,* name of the tractate, chapter, *mishnah.* There is an English translation in: H. Danby, *The Mishnah* (Oxford: Clarendon Press, 1933).
Meg	Tractate *Megila,* of the order *Mo'ed* of the *Mishnah.*
Men	Tractate *Menaḥot,* of the order *Qodashim* of the *Mishnah.*
Mid	Tractate *Midot,* of the order *Qodashim* of the *Mishnah.*
Ms.	Manuscript.
MT	(Proto-)Massoretic Text.
Nid	Tractate *Nida,* of the order *Tohorot* of the *Mishnah.*
NT	New Testament.
Ohol	Tractate *'Oholot ('Ahilut),* of the order *Tohorot* of the *Mishnah.*
OT	Old Testament.
par.	Parallel(s).
Pes	Tractate *Pesahim* (or *Pasha*), of the order *Mo'ed* of the *Mishnah.*
PG	*Patrologia Graeca,* ed. J.-P. Migne (Paris, 1857–1866).
Philo	*Philo in Ten Volumes (and Two Supplementary Volumes).* Greek text and English translation by F. H. Colson and G. H. Whitaker, in Loeb Classical Library (London–Cambridge, Mass.: William Heinemann–Harvard University Press). The classic English version by C. D. Yonge has been republished in a new updated edition with an introduction by David M. Scholer (Peabody, Mass.: Hendrickson Publishers, 1993).
Sanh	Tractate *Sanhedrin,* of the order *Neziqin* of the *Mishnah.*
Shab	Tractate *Shabbat,* of the order *Mo'ed* of the *Mishnah.*
Shebi	Tractate *Shebi'it,* of the order *Zera'im* of the *Mishnah.*
T . . .	(e. g., *TYoma* 4:2) *Tosefta,* name of the tractate, chapter, *halakha* (ed. Zuckermandel).
WT	Western Text.
Y . . .	(e.g., *YYoma* 2:4, p. 41c) *Jerusalem Talmud (Yerushalmi),* name of tractate, reference, folio, and column of the *editio princeps.*
Yeb	Tractate *Yebamot,* of the order *Nashim* of the *Mishnah.*

Introduction

As we begin the third Christian millennium, an obvious question to ask is, Where did Christianity come from? The obvious answer to this question is, of course, that Christianity came from Jesus. That is true, but only with some important qualifications. For if by Jesus we mean the Jesus who taught and healed in Galilee, the Jesus of the ministry, the attempt to attribute to him all the essential features of Christianity soon runs into serious difficulties.

First, there is a problem with our sources, specifically of knowing what there is in the Gospels that can be traced back personally to the Jesus of the ministry and not to a later community or redactor. The activities of the "Jesus Seminar" have been attracting a good deal of notoriety, but that is only one of the most recent phases of the so-called quest for the historical Jesus that has waxed and waned over the last two hundred or so years. Many New Testament experts, and consequently those who rely on their findings, are reluctant to attribute very much at all to the Jesus of the ministry. Now, if the underlying presupposition is that only what can be attributed to Jesus himself during his lifetime should be regarded as authentic Christianity, these results are dismaying. Among other consequences has been a widespread rejection of historical criticism of the Gospels by those who are concerned to preserve the integrity of Christian faith.

It is, of course, possible to question the methods and in particular the principles of the more radical critics. Many think that they often betray an unjustifiable degree of skepticism and mistrust

1

of their sources. But the problem lies much deeper. Even if we were sure of the authenticity of every one of Jesus' words and deeds recorded in the Gospels, we could still not attribute to the Jesus of the ministry all the essential features of Christianity. The most important element in Christianity that distinguishes and indeed divides it from Judaism is the admission of the Gentiles, regarded as a fulfillment of the Scriptures. It could be argued that the opening to the Gentiles, and even the establishment of communion between them and the original Jewish disciples of Jesus, was the most momentous act ever undertaken in the whole of Church history. Without it, Christianity—if indeed the term could then be used at all—would have remained an obscure Jewish sect.

But that event was totally unexpected and unforeseen. Luke recounts it in the story of the Roman centurion Cornelius, who sends a message to Peter to come to Caesarea (Acts 10:1–11:18). Peter can fall back on no word of Jesus to guide him at this point, not even, it seems, those words and gestures of Jesus that were later seen to point in the direction of the Gentiles. It is clear that the invitation and its implications—to stay in a Gentile's house and eat his food—are repugnant to him. It takes a vision twice repeated, with a heavenly word of interpretation and the express instruction of the Holy Spirit, to encourage him to go with the messengers. Worse still, at least according to St. Matthew's Gospel, Peter was going against an express command of Jesus given to those, including Peter, whom he was sending out on mission: "Do not make your way to Gentile territory, and do not enter any Samaritan town. Go rather to the lost sheep of the house of Israel" (Matt 10:5-6). Caesarea, it is true, was in Judea, so technically not in Gentile territory, although it was largely Gentile in character and population; but there is no indication that Peter resorted to any such subtlety in order to make up his mind to go to Cornelius, who, in any case, was not one of the lost sheep of the house of Israel.

At the end of Matthew's Gospel, we know, the risen Jesus commands his apostles to "make disciples of all nations" (Matt 28:19), thus implicitly revoking the earlier command, or rather declaring that it held good only for the time of the ministry. But that only makes the point clearer: it is the risen Jesus who opens the way to the Gentiles, and there is an important discontinuity with the Jesus of the ministry. Luke is implying the same when he attributes the opening to the Gentiles to the Holy Spirit.

That leads us immediately to another serious deficiency in the attempt to attribute Christianity simply to the Jesus of the ministry. It has the effect of trivializing the resurrection of Christ and the coming of the Spirit, reducing them to theological icing on the cake. Something of that is implied in the frequently heard terms contrasting the Jesus of history and the Christ of faith, as if the former were the real Jesus and the latter only what the Church has made of him. But in fact, for us who believe, who are Christians, the real Jesus is the risen Jesus, living, present, and active now in the Spirit and in the Church. We are not simply the followers of a long-dead Master, whose teachings we happen to find more true, more deep, or more inspiring than those of, say, the Buddha. Instead, we are members of his Body, animated by his Spirit, united in him with his Father. So we should not be scandalized or even surprised to realize that something new happened with Jesus' resurrection and as its consequence.

In fact, the very existence of Christianity, that is, of something that survived the death of Jesus, cannot be taken for granted. When the Jewish historian Josephus mentions Jesus toward the end of the first century, he indicates some surprise that what he calls the "tribe" or "breed" of Christians has outlasted its founder. The Pharisee Gamaliel, intervening in the trial of the apostles in Acts 5, compares the movement to those raised by Theudas and Judas the Galilean and supposes that, like them, this one too will fade away now that its initiator is dead.

Such remarks were not out of place. At the end of St. John's Gospel, the reaction of Peter and his companions, despite the extraordinary events they have just experienced, is to go back to their former occupation of fishing. The Jesus of the ministry does not seem to have organized more than a circle of disciples, and the apostles fled at the time of his arrest. Something did, however, continue, under the sign of the Spirit; according to Acts, it was set in motion at Pentecost, in a scene that gives concrete expression to the mission confided to the disciples by Christ after his resurrection.

What, then, were the origins of Christianity? What was the environment out of which the Christian Church emerged? What are the elements of continuity with that environment, and where precisely should we locate the rupture and the novelty?

This book is based on one written by the present writer and a colleague, Étienne Nodet, at the École Biblique in Jerusalem and entitled *The Origins of Christianity: An Exploration* (Collegeville, Minn.: The Liturgical Press [A Michael Glazier Book], 1998). It presents our main findings and principal arguments, though in a simpler and less technical form; for further information or documentation the reader is referred to that earlier book. Our approach is based on what might be called an analysis of institutions, which examines not so much what is said but the form in which it is said. That form is determined by a culture, and in particular by habitual ways of acting. Of special importance are rites, which constitute structures of meaning. These rites, we find, are the basic elements of continuity with the original environment. Put another way, they are the mnemonics that assure the function of memory. The novelty and rupture are expressed in the meanings that those rites now convey. What, more precisely, do we have in mind?

Christianity has always possessed two basic rites that complement each other, baptism and the Eucharist, the one giving access to the other. Our project has been to investigate the character of the early Christian community by looking into the origin of these two institutions. This, of course, has been done before. The originality of our inquiry consists in regarding baptism and the Eucharist as linked together. Put very simply, where do we find a religious culture in which these two rites are linked and play a central role? The result can be stated immediately: Christianity, we believe, emerged from an environment close to that of the Essenes. The Essenes, as described by Josephus and other ancient writers and revealed by the Qumran literature, practiced frequent ablutions for purification, in accordance with biblical legislation as well as their own customs. What gives them especial interest for our investigation is that in their system, certain significant ablutions ratified a process of initiation. This initiation gave access to a meal, which was the central action of the community. The meal consisted principally of bread and wine, taken in symbolic portions, and had an eschatological signification.

Within this marginal culture, a profound transformation came about, the decisive moment of which was contact with the Gentiles. The New Testament attributes that moment to the Spirit of the risen Jesus. It stands, in fact, in the very logic of the resurrection itself, for by rising from the dead, Jesus had transgressed the boundary between death and life. With that transgression, every other boundary fell that separated the impure from the pure, in particular that between Gentile and Jew. Life, goodness, and purity were no longer fragile, threatened and in need of being protected against death, evil, and impurity, which were perceived as stronger and ever menacing. Hostility could give way to hospitality, exclusion to communion. The result was an explosion, a cataclysm, that did not, however, destroy the group but opened it up to those whom it had never envisaged as members, and in so doing changed it—not quite beyond recognition. To be more precise, the institutional setting was preserved, as early Christian literature and even the modern liturgy attest. For rites are of their nature stable. At the same time, the meaning of those rites changed.

So, what was the original environment, which has just been described as being close to that of the Essenes? And who were the Essenes? We have known about the Essenes and similar groups from ancient times, principally from the writings of two Jewish authors of the first century A.D., the philosopher Philo of Alexandria and the historian Flavius Josephus, and also from the Roman writer Pliny the Elder. Within the last fifty years we have had access to a body of documents known as the Dead Sea Scrolls, which are generally regarded as the products of an Essene community living at or around the site of Qumran on the northwestern shore of the Dead Sea.

All this material, however, needs to be read with some caution. A quick reading of Philo and Josephus might give the impression that the Essenes were a single, homogeneous, even centrally organized body. But a closer reading of these authors reveals that the movement they describe admitted of many variations on a common theme and probably consisted of a great number of autonomous communities. For its part, the Qumran literature, which in any case is not all of a piece, both does and does not fit in with the literary data. Rather, "Essene"—which seems to mean "faithful"—was used as a sort of umbrella term coined by outsiders and covered numerous groups and subgroups. Viewed from the outside, these groups all looked much the same. They, no doubt, were intensely conscious of the variants, often minute, in customs and perhaps in doctrines that differentiated each from its rivals.

The religious culture of the Essenes was marginal and even sectarian. They stood apart from the Jerusalem Temple and its worship, which was the official center of Jewish religious and national life but which they regarded as polluted. No doubt they looked forward to a restored and purified Temple. In the meantime, however, their sacred meal was an act of priestly worship, and the room where it took place a sanctuary. Furthermore, each group regarded itself as the true Israel, charged exclusively with restoring the Covenant, and abominated others, that is, other Jews, as impure and wicked.

Josephus compares the Essenes to two other reform movements within contemporary Judaism, the Pharisees and the Sadducees. By implication, these had much in common with the Essenes, and yet they were distinct enough to be recognized as different even by outsiders. Josephus seeks to enlighten a Greek or Roman reader by comparing all three to schools of philosophy, with distinctive doctrines on points such as divine providence, human free will, and the reality and nature of life after death. Within Jewish culture, however, the similarities and the differences would have been appreciated in terms of practice rather than of theory.

The Essenes seem to have been distinguished principally by their way of life, which had a number of characteristic features, even allowing for internal variants, notably the long process of initiation into the community and the sacred meal reserved to members. As for the Pharisees, we are told by both the New Testament and Josephus that they followed "the traditions of the fathers"; the Sadducees, by contrast, took as their principle the Bible alone. The Pharisees seem to have been widely looked up to by other Jews, who did not necessarily follow all their rulings, and they became a point of reference in the reconstitution of Judaism that followed the national disasters of A.D. 70 and 135. The Sadducees, on the other hand, are described as exclusive and unpopular.

The Pharisees and the Sadducees, as we have just recalled, are mentioned in the New Testament; it has always been a good question why the Essenes are not. But if the original environment of Christianity was close to the Essenes, then we can immediately see why they would not be mentioned by name in the New Testament: the "insiders" would not use the term used by others to refer to them. Instead, the Gospels speak of "disciples"; this is close to the sense of Essenes as "faithful," namely to a Teacher ("Rabbi"), in this case John the Baptist or Jesus.

To return to our rites and institutions. It is not too difficult to establish notable parallels between baptism and the Eucharist, and the link between them, in the New Testament and other early Christian texts, on the one hand, and the customs of the Essenes and similar groups on the other. With these central rites go other practices, found both in the Acts of the Apostles and among the Essenes, which make up a coherent way of life, such as comparable procedures for accepting or excluding candidates for membership, officers with similar titles and functions, and analogous ways of practicing community of life and goods. In both cases we have a highly structured community, sure of its own identity and well marked off from others.

These similarities have often been noted. Such comparisons have multiplied since the discoveries at Qumran (although excessive attention has perhaps been given to the community occupying that site, and in particular to its apparently monastic features). Granted their reality and also their significance—that we are not simply dealing with a few random, superficial resemblances—only three explanations are possible. One is that these were general features of Second Temple Judaism. This explanation appears to gain weight from the undoubted fact that some of the characteristic practices common to early Christianity and the Essenes, including the most important, are to be found also in rabbinic Judaism, among them the baptism of converts ("proselytes") and the blessing of the cup and the bread in the Sabbath eve rite. Rabbinic Judaism claims to be the sole legitimate heir of Second Temple Judaism, so that its characteristic features are then assumed to be those generally found in Judaism two thousand years ago. But the distinctive features shared by the Essenes, by the first followers of Jesus, and by the earliest transmitters of the oral teaching that is the basis of rabbinic Judaism (the so-called Tannaites) have surprisingly little in common with the classic representations of first-century Judaism given by Philo and Josephus. So the occurrence in rabbinic Judaism of features shared with the Essenes and the followers of Jesus points rather to an original environment that was itself close to the Essenes, and therefore to Jesus' disciples, but equally distant from official circles.

The second explanation of the resemblances between the Church of the Acts of the Apostles and the Essenes is that the first Christians *borrowed* their structures from the Essenes. A variant form of this hypothesis is that converts from Essenism, perhaps flooding into the nascent Church in large numbers, brought these practices with them. That, however, is highly unlikely, since there is no trace of a conflict over these rites, as we might expect if they were novel to the original group. The true explanation is, therefore, that the disciples of Jesus were already used to these rites and structures. That is to say, the environment from which Christianity emerged was of Essene type.

A little earlier the rites and other institutions of Christianity were characterized as the mnemonics by which the Church remembers its origins. We still do today what Jesus and his disciples did. What they did was not invented by them but was part of the religious culture, marginal and sectarian in character, that they shared with other Essene-like groups. That still leaves untouched, of course, the question of the ultimate origins of these rites and institutions. They are not properly speaking biblical, even if there are obvious points of contact with biblical uses, such as that of water for purification. Instead, there are analogies with the practices of Greek fraternities of a "Pythagorean" type and with the way of life prescribed by Plato for the Guardians of the ideal city. Are these similarities purely accidental, or is there some real contact? There is a fine subject for future research.

In any case, if the rites show essential continuity of structure between Christianity and marginal, sectarian Judaism of Essene type, the meanings of those rites in Christianity express novelty and even rupture as well as continuity. Thus baptism still retains its function as a rite of initiation as well as its natural symbolism of purification. But it is already conferred in the nascent Church "in the name of Jesus," that is, invoking the presence and power of the Risen One (Acts 2:38, etc.; cf. 3:15-16). The apostle Paul, in his Epistle to the Romans, teaches that in being baptized we enter into the death and burial of Jesus Christ and into his resurrection and new life (see Rom 6:3-11). Similarly, the Eucharist is still the community meal of the Church, strictly reserved for the initiates (baptized). But the bread is now broken and eaten and the wine is drunk in memory of Jesus dead and risen.

AN OUTLINE OF THE BOOK

I. *Starting Points.* This first chapter deals with: (1) the sources of information; (2) two significant incidents in the New Testament: the baptism of Cornelius (Acts 10–11) and the "night at Troas" (Acts 20). These episodes bring baptism and the breaking of bread into sharper focus as customs dating back to earliest times.

II. *Baptism and Eucharist.* The central rites of Christianity are further explored. They are found to be characteristic of marginal sectarian groups to which the general label "Essene" has been attached. How did an exclusive group of this type become a worldwide Church open to all? Should we look to Galilee for the answer?

III. *Jewish Galilee.* Some modern studies of Christian origins assume that "Galilee of the Gentiles" was a likely setting for an opening to the non-Jewish world. On the contrary, rural Galilee was settled by Jews of a highly traditional observance who looked toward Babylonia as well as to Jerusalem. Some of these formed "fraternities," or communities of initiates; among them were militantly anti-Roman groups ("Galileans," "brigands," "zealots"). This was the environment from which Jesus and his first disciples came; it was also the environment that was later to be home to important rabbinical schools that later produced the Mishnah.

IV. *The Gentile Mission.* How then do we account for the Church's mission to the Gentiles? We look at the questions of Jewish proselytism and the God-fearers, at messianizing movements at Antioch ("where the disciples were first called 'Christians'"), Alexandria, and Rome. Paul and others preach that "the

Messiah is Jesus" to Jews in Asia Minor and Macedonia-Achaia. The result is conflict and persecution, which lead to new life and growth. "Turning to the Gentiles" is an effect of crisis in the Jewish communities and is perceived as the work of the Holy Spirit.

V. *James, Paul, and Peter.* By contrast, in Judea, from the Roman capture of Jerusalem in A.D. 70 to the failure of the second revolt under Bar Kokhba in 135, Jewish believers in Jesus in Judea were all observant Jews (the "Nazoreans"); James was their point of reference. What were their relations with Gentile believers in Jesus and with other Jews? We examine the implications of the "Jerusalem decrees" in the Book of Acts and the problem of the "sectaries" *(minim).* We trace the formation of rabbinic Judaism, seeing its development as different fraternities are federated into a comprehensive system that consequently allowed for various schools. At the same time, New Testament Christianity is formed around the agreement between Peter and Paul, not excluding James and including also John.

VI. *The Covenant.* We take up again some questions left hanging from earlier chapters: the paschal lamb; Passover and Easter; Pentecost and the Covenant; admission and exclusion; and finally, why the name *christiani* stuck to Jesus' disciples.

VII. *And Jesus?* In the light of all this, what can we say about Jesus and his ministry? What did his contemporaries think of him?

Note: In relating this book to the earlier one on which it is based, the reader should know that the first two chapters of both correspond. Chapter 3 of this book contains material from chapters 3, 4, and the first part of chapter 5 of *The Origins of Christianity* (see p. 4). Chapter 4 of this book corresponds to chapter 6 of *Origins.* Chapters 5 and 6 of this book contain material from chapters 5 and 7, respectively, of *Origins.* Chapter 7 of this book is new. This book also takes account of some further reflection on the part of *The Origins of Christianity* since the publication of the latter.

Some final comments. The whole tendency of this work runs counter to a certain widespread idea about the rise of Christianity and precisely the origins of the Church. According to this, Christianity arose as an unstructured or only very loosely structured movement of enthusiasts gathered around a charismatic figure. After his disappearance this enthusiasm was sustained by the conviction of a number of leading members that he had risen from the dead and that he would shortly return to usher in the last times. When he failed to do so after a reasonable interval, these same members began to organize the movement into what would eventually become the Christian Church, with structures, sacraments, and dogmas borrowed from various external sources. On the contrary, we find that the structural elements belong to the original environment itself. They did not have to be invented or imported.

The Christianity that emerges from our study is very Jewish in its institutions, including its sacraments and dogmas. In recent times it has become customary to say that Jesus was Jewish, which, of course, is quite true, even though some misleading conclusions have been drawn about what that may have meant in concrete reality. At the same time, it has also been usual to say that Christianity is not Jewish but at best a hybrid with some "Jewish roots," whose divergence from rabbinic Judaism—tacitly supposed to be normative—is all on the side of Christianity. Furthermore, what are then regarded as its non-Jewish features, especially its sacraments and dogmas, are taken to originate in the Hellenistic world, from mystery religions and the like.

On the contrary, we find that the most characteristic features of Christianity, including the Eucharist, the Trinity, and the sign of the cross, are, *as institutions,* Jewish, even if their meaning has changed. If indeed it can be shown that this or that element does have its origin in the Hellenistic world, it comes to Christianity via Judaism, in which it has already been domesticated. The novelty of Christianity consists in a single but all-important point: it is the proclamation that, through Jesus' death and resurrection, divine judgment has already been passed on the world, and there is a new creation.

From the same or a similar sectarian Jewish environment in the first century, there emerged what became two religions: Christianity, claiming to be the universalist fulfillment of Judaism, and rabbinic Judaism, claiming to represent the nation. It follows that the historic quarrel between Christianity and Judaism—let us be more precise, rabbinic Judaism—is a family quarrel. But then such quarrels are always the most bitter. "A certain man had two sons . . . ." "Make my brother give me a share of our inheritance . . . ." The Book of Genesis is written from the point of view of Isaac and Jacob; we are given only occasional glimpses of how Ishmael and Esau may have seen things. The New Testament claims an inheritance, which the Talmud implicitly denies.

Chapter One

Starting Points

I. THE SOURCES

In the first part of this chapter, we shall look at the main sources, Christian and Jewish, of our study of the origins of Christianity. First, we need to be clear about a few general points.

In the case of any text, we can make a distinction between its composition and its publication, that is, the moment when it escapes from the control of the author or group that produced it. Before the invention of printing, when copies had to be made by hand, a text could be said to be published when it became available for copying. This might have meant depositing a fair copy in a public library or giving it to a bookseller, a friend, a patron, or other individual, who could then lend it to others to read and copy.

A further distinction lies in the difference between the publication of a text and its authority. This difference is often hard to appreciate, for the authority of a text is initially derived from the reputation of those responsible for it. At a certain point, however, the *text itself* may come to be regarded as authoritative. For the biblical writings, a further moment occurred with their canonization, that is, their incorporation into the official list of texts that were recognized as normative and even inspired. On the other hand, further alteration and reworking cannot be totally excluded after publication or even after canonization. Thus the text of the Hebrew Bible continued to evolve long after its translation into Greek.

1. THE NEW TESTAMENT

a) *New Testament and Kerygma*

This is not the place to discuss the literary origins of the various books of the NT but rather to study what use the first Christians made of them. Irenaeus, at the end of the second century, was able to describe and defend something like the NT as we know it. By his time, therefore, a body of Christian writings was acknowledged as having the status of Scripture.

The earlier position of Christian writers was quite different. Ignatius of Antioch, at the beginning of the second century, sums up their attitude when he declares: "My documents are Jesus Christ; my unimpeachable documents are his cross and resurrection, and the faith that comes from him" (*Letter to the Philadelphians* 8). So even if the composition of the books that form the NT was already well under way, there was as yet no *written* authoritative reference point. Ignatius speaks often of Christ but refers to precise events only in succinct statements which are very close to the primitive *kerygma,* that is, the proclamation of the saving death and resurrection, or which resemble those of the "Apostles'" Creed. He is therefore in the same situation as Paul, whom he knows as a writer but whom he never quotes. On the other hand, he is well aware what a normative text is, since he knows and cites the OT, which he interprets typologically, thus assuring the continuity between the two covenants.

Fifteen years earlier, Clement of Rome made much use of the OT, fairly freely and most of the time, it seems, from memory. Sometimes he attributed the status of Scripture to texts that have since been lost or to received interpretations of biblical passages. As Christian Scripture he knows at most Paul's First Letter to the Corinthians and recalls the context of crisis in which it was written. He refers often to salvation in Jesus Christ, but, like Ignatius, without ever alluding to the facts of the life of Jesus. Only once does he cite words of Jesus (*Letter to the Corinthians* 13:2), but the saying is not known in this form in the NT; so for Clement there is no *official* text (although that does not, of course, exclude the existence of some documents). He speaks of Jesus only by way of the OT. Thus, when speaking of Christ as the suffering servant, he makes no direct reference to his life but uses only a biblical passage, the song of Isaiah 53:1-12 (as does Hebrews 10:5 with Psalm 40:7 LXX).

This absence of normative Christian writing is confirmed by the ways in which the gospel was transmitted. The *Didache,* or *Teaching of the Twelve Apostles,* encourages respect for the one who proclaims the word of God (4:1), recommends the company of the saints, who are faithful witnesses, and warns against false teachers. Polycarp speaks of fidelity to the word handed down by tradition since the beginning, which makes it possible to refute those who deny the incarnation. For the *Shepherd* of Hermas, false prophets can only be detected by their way of life. Papias, bishop of Hierapolis at the time of Ignatius and Polycarp, is known only through Eusebius (*Ecclesiastical History* 3.39.1-7), who says that Papias made inquiry concerning the *words* of the apostles, who are named but without indicating any evangelist; Papias insisted that the oral tradition was more useful to him than any writings. Eusebius thus confirms the direct sources, and his testimony concerning Papias is all the more significant in that he disapproves of what he regards as the latter's lack of respect for the NT.

With Justin, in the mid-second century, things have changed. According to the *First Apology* 67.3, the books about Jesus, referred to as "memoranda of the apostles," are read, together with the works of the prophets, at the Sunday assembly. The new state of affairs has a double aspect: there are now Christian texts of reference, and Justin, though still adhering to the primacy of the traditional (oral) kerygma, makes many allusions to the life of Jesus and takes pains to situate his sayings in a narrative context. However, the quotations do not exactly match the Gospels as we know them, and these "memoranda of the apostles" seem to be a Gospel harmony in a form earlier than that attested by Tatian's *Diatessaron;* the elements of which it is composed come from the canonical Gospels, but at an archaic stage of their development. In the *Dialogue with Tryphon,* the term "Scripture(s)" always designates the OT, which is at the center of the debate. Justin, however, interprets it through Gospel traditions of several kinds: collections of sayings of Jesus, but without context; episodes obviously inspired by the Gospel accounts, especially concerning John the

Baptist, the nativity, and the passion; explicit references to the "memoranda," which, according to Justin, Tryphon, though a Jew, could have consulted. Compared with the writers who preceded him, Justin attests two salient facts. One is the existence of Christian writings that are regulative, though they do not yet have the stature of incontestable Scripture (and it is not clear how far, in terms of territory, their authority extends). The other is the complete absence of any reference to Paul or Acts, which would suggest that the canon has not yet been fixed.

From all this it emerges that the appearance of authoritative Christian writings, as distinct from the works of individual Christians, followed well behind the oral transmission of the kerygma. This is still the state of things at the time of Irenaeus. For him, the tradition has four phases, to be carefully distinguished: the prophets have announced, Christ has established, the apostles have handed on, and the Church hands on throughout the entire world (*Demonstration of the Apostolic Preaching* 99). The first three terms designate the three classes of writings in the usual biblical order: OT, Gospels, Epistles. In his work *Against the Heresies*, Irenaeus thinks in terms of a structure that is alternately binary (OT/NT), in accordance with the tradition of typological exegesis, and ternary, by distinguishing the Lord from the apostles, that is, the Gospels from the rest of the NT. However, the written text is not everything for him, for he accuses Marcion of manipulating the Gospel texts or simply of giving too much attention to the letter, to the detriment of a global view of the single gospel, in relation to which the four booklets called Gospels are only particular aspects (*Against the Heresies* 1.27.2). It goes without saying that his protest against abuse of the written word presupposes that authoritative texts were in existence.

Behind these debates and hesitations lies a central problem. If Jesus is regarded primarily as a teacher, then what he taught and the principal facts of his life will be of the highest importance. If, on the other hand, the emphasis is placed on the kerygma, with the proclamation of the cross and resurrection at its heart, then the biography of Jesus assumes less importance; that does not, of course, exclude other, even precise, recollections of Jesus' ministry. The long time it took for the canonical Gospels to emerge may even suggest that it was thought dangerous to *publish* the biography of Jesus. Note that, at the time of Justin or Irenaeus, the Gospels had only been recently composed. No doubt there were written documents from the earliest times, but with the status of private notes, which explains why their texts remained somewhat fluid throughout the second century. It is quite possible that the *harmony* attested by Justin was the trace of a first (abortive) attempt at publishing a text of reference, at least for internal use, in the form of a synthesis of venerable notes possessing apostolic authority. In any case, the documents that resulted in the canonical Gospels continued to evolve after the harmony was put together.

These remarks lead to useful consequences for our task, which is to identify the environment from which the apostles went out on mission. First, if what is spoken and heard, rather than what is written, is primary, there follow relations of master and disciple and so questions of obedience. In its turn, the act of writing also implies a control, hence the various stages of canonization or revision of texts; during this process, ancient translations may have escaped revision and so may witness to an earlier state of the Greek text. Finally, regarding the biographies of Jesus, that is, the Gospels, their publication supposes that they are in agreement with the kerygma—in other words that the Jesus whom their reader encounters is not simply the Teacher but the Risen One. That implies that they have undergone reworking inspired by the preaching of cross and resurrection, although the Teacher has left his traces in the text.

b) *The Acts of the Apostles*

The Acts of the Apostles is one of our most important sources for the study of Christian origins. Interesting questions arise concerning its text. In fact, there appear to be two relatively distinct forms of the entire book. One of these has been known since the eighteenth century as the "Western Text" (henceforth WT), since two of its principal witnesses—a major Greek manuscript (*Codex Bezae,* referred to under the sign D) and the Old Latin translation—are of Western origin. Other constant witnesses to this type of text are ancient versions in Syriac, Coptic, and Ethiopian. Readings of a Western type are to be found as well in ancient liturgical books and the writings of certain Fathers of the Church, especially Irenaeus. The name "Western Text" is therefore misleading, but we shall continue to use it for its convenience. The other text-type, whose principal witness is *Codex Vaticanus* (ms. B), can fittingly be called "Alexandrian" (henceforth AT). The distinctions that we made a little earlier between composition, publication, and canonization make it possible to see how two types of the same text could remain in circulation at the same time, even within a fairly restricted environment where the text was regarded as authoritative but not yet as definitive.

The relationship between these two text-types has long been the subject of speculation. As early as the seventeenth century, the suggestion was made that Luke published two editions of Acts. Most scholars today hold that the WT is secondary to the AT and originated essentially in explanatory glosses (ms. D is longer than the standard text given by the majority of Greek manuscripts). This consensus has, however, been challenged, notably by two French Dominican scholars, M.-E. Boismard and A. Lamouille, who have tried to restore the WT not only from *Codex Bezae* but also from the other witnesses that frequently seem to translate or quote a Greek text earlier than that given by the majority of Greek manuscripts. This restored text, they argue, represents the Book of Acts as written by Luke; the AT, on the contrary, results from an important revision of the earlier version.

In the course of our investigation of Christian origins, direct comparison between the restored WT and AT of Acts will turn out to be highly profitable. Many small differences, which are easily passed over or regarded as mere accidents of textual transmission, take on a new interest once the WT is held to be earlier, whereas the opposite hypothesis can see in them only insignificant variants or marks of careless editing. In particular, the AT, viewed as a final revision, suggests how Acts was reworked to make it conform to the realities of a later period in the life of the Church or to the conceptions that the Church then had of its own past. Following back down the line of successive reworkings of the narrative, we may even be able to recover some missing links in the history of the origins of Christianity.

2. QUMRAN DOCUMENTS AND RABBINIC TEXTS

These two collections are very different from each other. They do, however, have one thing in common: they were not intended to be published. In the case of Qumran, there is a reforming sect, access to which is strictly controlled. Among the rabbis, emphasis is placed on the oral tradition, and so on the relationship of master and disciple. It is worth pointing out that the whole of rabbinic literature is pretty well unintelligible for an unprepared *reader* with all the good will in the world: it takes for granted an oral teaching. We shall be able to put this common feature, namely esoteric teaching, into a context when we have taken a look at each of the two groups in turn.

a) *The Qumran Documents*

Josephus describes the Essenes as one party among others in Judaism. Viewed from within, their intention is at once more precise and more ambitious. In the *Community Rule* (1 QS), found at Qumran, the members are to separate themselves from perverse folk and begin by going into the desert in order to rediscover the practice of the "first ordinances" (8:1-16a and 9:3–10:8a); thus it is a return to the sources, that is, to the gift of the Law at Sinai in the desert. At the same time an esoteric side is stressed: the doctrines must be hidden from the perverse (9:12f.), that is, from anyone who does not belong to the group. The belief that the community alone has the true Covenant (5:8, 20; 6:15) is expressed in liturgical worship, which had an eschatological dimension, as in the *Appendix to the Rule* or *Rule of the Congregation* (1 QSa) and the *Temple Scroll* (11 QT).

The observance laid down is defined in relation to the Law of Moses, but mediated by "what the prophets have revealed by the Holy Spirit": the community—and it alone—has the inspired interpretation, in continuity with the prophets. In other words, the Law comprises two domains: laws that are clear and transparent, explicit in Scripture and accessible to all, and laws that are hidden and can be correctly interpreted only by the community. The interpretation in question is indeed *scriptural*, but divinely inspired and taking account of changing circumstances. These laws remain internal and are handed on by the masters, so they are not, properly speaking, published. This means that the texts found in the caves near Qumran should be regarded as essentially private and incomplete memoranda, not as published works, which may explain why many of the non-biblical documents among them do not have the appearance of finished products. Still, they have been carefully preserved, which would show that they were regarded as important. Finally, among the solemn engagements undertaken by those admitted by the Essenes as new members, according to Josephus, is an oath not to divulge anything concerning the community (*J.W.* 2 §141).

The central element on which the precepts proper to the group converge is the "purity," which is nothing other than a community meal taken in very strict conditions of purity. In the same way, the ancestors of the rabbinic tradition are defined as eating profane food in a state of Levitical purity. This provides an intrinsic link that we will develop later on.

b) *The Rabbinic Texts*

In the rabbinic tradition, the Torah, which is for "all Israel," comprises the written text and the oral tradition, the two pillars of which are the Pentateuch and the Mishnah respectively. The ultimate purpose of the Torah and the precepts is the acceptance of the "yoke of the kingdom of heaven" and the "yoke of the commandments," which *liberates* from the yoke of nature. The point of departure is expressed at the beginning of the tractate *'Abot*: "Moses received the Torah from Sinai, then transmitted it . . . ." Thus Sinai appears as an absolute beginning, both for the written and for the oral instruction.

The oral Torah is sometimes thought of as a commentary on the Pentateuchal legislation. That idea, however, is misleading. The oral Torah originated in an unwritten tradition that was only later related to the Bible; the rabbinic tradition itself acknowledges that not all the branches of the oral Torah are equally well founded on Scripture. The distinction between written Torah and oral Torah, both having equal rank, appears clearly for the first time with Hillel and Shammai, a little before Christ. This is the period in which, again according to rabbinic tradition, the internal controversies begin. Nowhere are the doctors said to be "inspired," except perhaps collectively.

The internal unity of the Torah finds expression only in the oneness of God who gave it. Nowhere is it expressed in terms of a *logical* coherence, which would amount to subordinating God to rational human thought. Outside homiletics there is no trace of any attempt to reduce everything to simple principles, not even to the Decalogue (Ten Commandments), which is nevertheless the charter of the Covenant at Sinai (see Exod 19–20). According to tradition, the Torah contains 613 precepts; they are not specified, but the important thing to note is that they are not put in any hierarchical order.

The differences between the rabbis and the Essenes are obvious. Yet the method of handing on teaching that is proper to the Tannaites, the early transmitters of the rabbinic tradition, allows a comparison to be made. The body of oral laws, or Mishnah in the broad sense, has been known since the third century in written form. In the first centuries of our era it was not supposed to be written down; yet we are told that the doctors wrote down all or part of the Mishnah for their private use. Their teachings were placed in the public domain, at least within the academy, by what amounted to an oral publication: once they were fixed, they were memorized and transmitted by "repeaters" *(Tannaim).*

3. PHILO AND JOSEPHUS

The lives of Philo and Josephus span the first century of the Christian era. One was a philosopher, the other a historian, but what they had in common was the intention to spread public knowledge of Scripture, duly provided with commentary, that is, to disseminate a tradition without any control over the reader. In both cases the author was an important and well-known person but neither has left any following that can be traced to him.

a) *Philo of Alexandria* (d. A.D. 45)

Philo's outlook is very different from that of the first Christians. For him, the Bible, or more exactly the Pentateuch, is not first and foremost a code but a book of philosophy giving access to truth, which exists in the world of ideas. The Law of Moses, or *nomos*, is the law of the world and has the unity of a rational discourse, or *logos*; for that reason it begins with Creation. This view has Stoic roots but is attached to the utopia of a future ideal city. In this sense Philo is heir to Hellenism, which, from the time of Alexander the Great, sought to reduce the sphere of "barbarism" through cultural expansion. It follows that only the one who observes the Law is truly an inhabitant of the world, or *cosmopolitēs*. Further, it is necessary to show the profound unity of the Law, which Philo does by trying to bring everything back to the Decalogue (we immediately observe an important difference from the rabbinic tradition). Philo envisages the spread of the Law of Moses to the rest of humanity through waves of Jewish emigration and now by his own writings.

These views are obviously far removed from the outlook of the first disciples of Jesus, who at first had no overall program, as we shall see at greater length. Their mission expanded only through opposition and persecution, as even the final synthesis of Acts (governed by 1:8) brings out clearly. Moreover, their idea was not to spread the Law of Moses (see Acts 15:21) but to proclaim an event, beginning with the Jews. On the other hand, it is easy to foresee how, during a phase of reflection following the unplanned beginnings, Philo could be of help in interpreting the development of Christianity.

b) *Flavius Josephus* (d. ca. A.D. 100)

Josephus, in the preface to his *Jewish Antiquities* (1 §3), explains that it is necessary to publish certain important facts that are useful to know, such as those recorded in "the sacred library." What that contains is not mythology, even though it goes back much earlier in time than the Greek historians (1 §§22f.). But the Law of Moses does not in fact date from the beginnings, since it came on the scene at a much later point in history. In the prologue, Josephus tries hard to get round the difficulty in several ways. First he invokes the antiquity of Moses, "born two thousand years ago, at a time so remote that the poets have not even dared to put back that far the birth of the gods, let alone the deeds of men and their laws" (*Ant.* 1 §16). After this side step, which brings Moses close to the beginnings and places him before the known civilizations, Josephus explains that in fact the Law and the political constitution that flows from it are the fruit of Moses' meditation on the nature of God and his works.

Such a view fits in well with a rigorous monotheism but leaves little room for anything specific to Israel. So there is a contradiction that Josephus cannot escape: if God has expressed himself entirely in Creation, then notions of Covenant, promise, election, which are nothing if not historical, become problematic, and Josephus quietly drops them. As a result, in contrast to Philo, he has no clear teaching about spreading the Law throughout the world and is somewhat bothered by the fact that the best of political constitutions, divinely inspired, is not that of Rome, the best of empires.

Josephus has a number of contacts with the NT: the census of Quirinius, the differences between the Pharisees and Sadducees, the uprisings of Judas the Galilean and Theudas, Felix, Festus, Agrippa, Drusilla, Berenice, etc. These contacts raise the question of some sort of dependence or common source but do not conceal the fact that his perspective is profoundly different, since he sets aside any notion of historical revelation and systematically discredits anything to do with messianism.

Both Philo and Josephus insist on the teaching and study of the Law. Josephus points out several times that one of the characteristics of the Pharisees is the observance of "ancestral customs," which are not derived from Scripture, and he states that he himself is attached to this party. But when he expounds the Law, the sole authority that he indicates is the Bible. To be exact, he mentions many non-biblical usages, some of which are to be found in the rabbinic tradition, but he never suggests that he has any source other than the written instruction. One reason for this attitude may be a desire to show that the Jewish Law is really ancient, but at the same time transparent and accessible to all, with no esoteric domain (see *Ant.* 3 §318).

For his part, Philo first remarks that the patriarchs before Moses are incarnations of the Law: the true sage is the one who knows how to govern without relying on any written text, that is, without any external precept. Moses is at once king, priest, and prophet, or even a "living law endowed with speech." In other words, for Philo the "unwritten law," universal and in conformity with nature, is innate and does not come from outside by way of tradition. This conception is the opposite of the central importance given to the oral tradition by the Pharisees or rabbis, which is not only positive but also inaccessible outside the relationship of master and disciple.

4. CONCLUSIONS

By way of the criteria of publication and publicity, these brief sketches show a very clear difference between Philo and Josephus on the one hand, and Essenes and Tannaites on the other. It is really a difference of *nature*, more important than any agreements or disagreements in respect to content. In fact, behind the question of oral teaching or publication lies another: in the Bible, Creation is fundamentally a work of separation and organization, and the maintenance of clear boundaries is essential for the notions of election and Covenant. Even to translate the Bible poses a serious problem. From this point of view, the work of Philo and Josephus belongs to a new kind of literature—apologetic—whether philosophical or historical. They address whoever wishes to read them, with the very clear idea that the Law of Moses, being the best of all, should be known and should inspire every lawgiver.

By contrast, the Essenes and the rabbis, taken together, with their oral teaching, are more traditional, since they accentuate the relationship between master and pupil (supported by repetition in the course of worship, where the *Shema' Israel* already sets out the program; see Deut 6:4ff.). Their characteristic feature is to take oral teaching to an absolute limit; the only instruction that exists is oral, not to be divulged to outside circles.

In which category should the NT be placed? Once the canon is established, it becomes a book, as public in legal standing as in content, with a message for all. Part of its content consists of legislation, which presupposes a society (the kingdom) with well-defined boundaries, within which "whatever you bind will be bound, whatever you loose will be loosed" (cf. Matt 16:19 and 18:18). On the other hand, in Luke's prologue, Theophilus is not just any reader but a member of the community who has heard the preaching; so what is put before the public is a literature that was originally internal. In the final phase of development, it is appropriate to make a certain comparison with Philo and Josephus. However, in the first generations (at least until Irenaeus), the oral aspect was predominant: not only did Jesus write nothing, but his biography remained subordinate to the preaching.

The oral aspect of Christianity lasted after the movement opened up to the Gentiles, but that does not imply that it was secret. Even if there was not yet an official biography of Jesus, Christians wrote on their own responsibility, and their writings—not only the NT epistles but many other texts—were distributed, apparently without limitation. Justin, in his *Apology*, even addresses the emperor Antoninus, the Senate, and the whole Roman people. Teaching was both public and oral, with some precautions in time of persecution. There was certainly no Christian *arcanum* comparable to the secret cult of the mysteries; it was not until the third century that the organization of the catechumenate entailed a difference of publicity in preaching and worship, with only the initiates being admitted to knowledge of the customs. On the other hand, a distinction should be made between preaching to all and the activities proper to the community, since it is clear that, from the beginning, access to the rites was protected, as we shall see later.

Finally, it is worth pointing out that the NT as we have it, and especially the Gospels, is entirely dependent on that branch of Jesus' disciples, gathered around Peter and Paul, which is centered on the kerygma of the resurrection. The Acts of the Apostles has preserved a few traces of other groups: Apollos and the disciples at Ephesus, who know only the baptism of John, represent at least one other current, which must have lived on with its own teaching; a similar observation could be made on the subject of James, to whom even Peter gives an account of himself.

Little is known about the later history of Jewish believers, but their biography of Jesus (the *Gospel of the Hebrews*), which apparently was not published, would have presented a rather different picture from the one we know, even if the facts related were more or less the same. There are traces of such a picture in the NT, but they have been almost obliterated by a final redaction that has a different orientation. Similar traces are to be found also in the Eastern Churches, which regard themselves as the heirs of Jude, Thomas, etc., although nothing in the NT would lead us to suspect that. We shall return to some of these points in chapter 5.

II. TWO INTRIGUING EPISODES

From what has been seen in the previous section, it is clear that the Gospels are not the best place to look for the origins of Christianity, that is to say, for what happened immediately after Jesus left the scene. Two reasons for this have emerged: the delay in *publishing* the biography of Jesus and the almost total silence regarding rites and structures. In Acts, however, we find two episodes that get around these pitfalls and enable us to glimpse the environment revealed by the first steps of the apostles.

1. PETER AND CORNELIUS

This famous scene is certainly important, given its length and repetitions, whereas the few other episodes in the mission of Peter are reported only briefly. This narrative (Acts 10:1-48) tells of a visit to a Gentile, something new and risky, since Peter has to justify himself afterward (Acts 11:1-18) and cannot appeal to a tradition going back to Jesus. This simple observation raises the hope that the event will throw light both on the environment of the first community *and* on Jesus' own horizon.

This narrative contains a number of remarkable features:

1. The Book of Acts attributes the first movement toward the Gentiles to several agents: here to Peter (foreshadowed by Philip in Samaria and with the Ethiopian in Acts 8); to anonymous preachers coming from Cyprus and Cyrene to Antioch (Acts 11:20, according to the WT); to Paul, and on several occasions, at Antioch of Pisidia (Acts 13:46), at Corinth (Acts 18:6), and at Rome (Acts 28:28). The narrative of Peter and Cornelius is a sort of paradigm of the entire development.

2. The presentation of "Cornelius, centurion of the Italic cohort, pious and fearing God, as all his household, giving generous alms to the Jewish people" (Acts 10:1-2) shows an important person of the best category, as close as possible to Judaism, yet who, as a Gentile, is separated by a barrier that cannot be crossed. So it is highly significant—and stretching the bounds of probability—to put on center stage an officer of the army of occupation, who as such professes an emperor worship incompatible with Judaism (see Matt 8:8 par.), and to have him pass directly to Christianity without first entering Judaism through circumcision. The objection of the Pharisees (Acts 15:5) thus bears on an extreme case.

3. The Spirit is shown openly at the beginning and end of the narrative: at Peter's departure for Caesarea and in the house of his hosts. As he later says to the brethren (Acts 11:15), he recognizes that the same thing has happened to them as to "us at the beginning." So there is a communion between "them" and "us." In Acts 4:31 the apostles receive the Spirit while they are gathered together, but without any identifiable chronological link with Pentecost. On that occasion they are given an assurance that enables them to testify with power to the resurrection of Jesus as an event that shakes the foundations.

4. In fact, the resurrection of Jesus amounts to a very serious tampering with boundaries, since the necessary separation between life and death, represented respectively by the pure and the impure, is thus compromised. It is comparable to the violation involved in Peter's communion with Gentiles (impure) and is even its model, since it is provoked by the same Spirit. In other episodes the Spirit is manifested by "tongues," an ambiguous phenomenon that can represent either the overthrow of the rules of language (nonsense, drunkenness; see Acts 2:13f.) or communication beyond linguistic barriers. Indeed, the earthquake of Acts 4:31 introduces a cosmic dimension, and the whole problem is to know if these transgressions are a return to primitive chaos before Creation, itself an act of separation and organization, or if they can be compared to a new creation (see Gen 1:2: "And the spirit of God brooded over the waters"). Peter's vision of *all* the animals proceeds from a similar

idea: Creation in its diversity, but without separation between clean and unclean.

5. Peter's reaction to the manifestation of the Spirit is to have the Gentiles "baptized." At first sight this seems to be simply an order to go to the ritual bath. But then, what could such a gesture signify? They already have the Spirit and so are deemed to be pure, and Peter stays and eats with them. When he asks, "Can anyone refuse?" he is implicitly replying to the objection that baptism is unthinkable for such folk. Apparently that is because they are not Jewish, since the convert Pharisees will demand that these Gentiles be circumcised. So it is clear that the newcomers to the group to whom Peter is accustomed, namely Jews, get baptized. In other words, baptism marks the entry into the group.

In the incident at Caesarea, baptism is "in the name of Jesus," which implies that the gesture of immersion is capable of more than one meaning. But if what is referred to here is just an isolated act of immersion with no mention of an officiant, it is not easy to see in what sense it can be performed "in the name of Jesus."

The underlying question is really much wider. We need to see if the term "baptism" used here does not in fact refer to a whole procedure, with a certain number of steps and rites, in which case Peter's order would amount to the admission of the household as candidates to follow this course. In any case, what Peter has to say invites us to give close attention to the nature of John's baptism, all the more as Jesus himself was a baptizer, as were at least some of his disciples (see John 3:22). What is the connection between the baptism received and conferred by Jesus and his disciples and baptism "in the name of Jesus"?

6. The sole biblical category into which baptism (immersion) can be placed is purification. For the rabbinic tradition there is an impurity inherent in Gentiles that has the same force as the impurity of one who has a seminal discharge; it is spread by contact, and what the person touches is contaminated as well (see Lev 15:1-18). That means it is serious, and of a kind that is invariable and does not depend on any particular contamination, such as that of a corpse (see *TOhol* 1:4). The tradition is aware that this impurity is not in origin biblical (*TNida* 9:14). It is important to note

that the same principle is found among the Essenes (1 QM 9:8f.) and in Matthew 18:16, where, after formal warnings have gone unheeded, the stubborn offender is excluded from the community: to be regarded as "a Gentile or a publican" means to be impure, so that all contact becomes impossible. These notions are in complete contrast with the views of Philo and Josephus, who never mention any impurity attaching to Gentiles as such.

As for going into a Gentile's house, even without touching anything, the Mishnah (*MOhol* 18:7) explains that it is forbidden, because it is to be presumed that fetuses have been buried under the floor or in the walls, and under a roof the impurity of a corpse spreads by convection, even without contact (generalizing Num 19:14-15).

From all this it emerges that Peter and the brethren, within the original environment, could have had no idea at all of proselytism among the Gentiles: it took the impetus of the Spirit to break down the barriers. As for conversion to Judaism, the Pharisees (in our narrative) allow it, since they demand the circumcision of those Gentiles who have become Christian (perhaps as the lesser of two evils). But it is not certain that Peter and his companions would have spontaneously allowed it, which may explain why their reaction was not to circumcise the newcomers.

But we can go further. The fact that *Jewish* newcomers to the group were admitted by a rite of baptism implies that they, too, were previously impure. At least in this context, circumcision did not count or was not enough.

2. THE NIGHT AT TROAS

What was the meaning of the "breaking of the bread," which recurs periodically in Acts as a regular activity of the community? Nowhere is this rite described, but one passage supplies some important details: the night-long vigil at Troas in Asia Minor (Acts 20:7-12), when Paul restores the young Eutychus, who has fallen from a window on the third level. This scene has been attached to Paul's third missionary journey, centering on Ephesus (see also Acts 16:8-11, from his second journey). The following is a literal translation, showing some interesting textual variants.

(**20**:6) *As for us, we set sail from Philippi after the days of Un-leavened Bread and came to Troas in five days and stayed for seven days. (7) The first day of the week, while we had come to-gether to break the bread, Paul was debating with them, before leaving the next day; he prolonged his speech until the middle of the night. (8) There were many lamps* (the WT has *lights*) *in the upper room where we had met. (9) A young man by name Euty-chus, seated on the window ledge, being overcome by a heavy sleep while Paul was speaking, fell down from the third level and was taken up dead. (10) Paul went down, threw himself on him and taking him in his arms said: "Do not be troubled, his soul* (or *his life) is in him." (11) Having gone up again and broken bread and eaten and talked a good while until dawn, thus he departed.*

(12)	WT: (12) *While they were embracing one another,*
They took the child alive and they were consoled beyond measure.	*he took the young man alive, and they were consoled beyond measure.*

Several aspects of this narrative call for commentary:

1. Just as Peter had raised up Tabitha, the woman disciple of Joppe (Acts 9:36-42), so Paul raises up Eutychus, with many bib-lical overtones. As with the approach to the Gentiles, the two apostles are thus on equal footing. Commentators associate the raising of Eutychus with the breaking of the bread on the first day of the week, commemorating the resurrection of Jesus. But what is the origin of this rite? It is not easy to see how we get to the as-sembly at Troas from the narratives of the Last Supper in the Syn-optic Gospels. The setting there is Passover. Jesus announces his death, and, at first sight, there is no connection with the resurrec-tion on the first day of the week. The only common element is the breaking of the bread, and the problem is to see how this gesture could have been derived from the annual Passover meal, even supposing that the bread in question is unleavened. As the other occurrences of the "breaking of the bread" give no further clarifi-cation, the problem will have to be looked at in the next chapter from the angle of the Last Supper.

2. The episode takes place on the night of the first day of the week, that is, between Saturday and Sunday. The final text of the night at Troas mentions the presence of many "lamps" (v. 8), an odd, isolated detail when nothing else is said concerning the arrangement of the room. The WT speaks instead of "lights," in the sense of high windows or skylights, which has some connection with the narrative, since Eutychus falls from a window. Why the change, which only makes the account less coherent?

In fact, lamps on a Saturday evening do have a well-attested meaning in a Jewish context. Latin satirists (Seneca, Persius Flaccus) rail against idleness and smoking lamps on the Sabbath among the Jews of Rome. They cannot have meant the lighting of lamps on Friday evening, since the Romans counted the day from midnight to midnight, and in any case, the Jews could only light lamps before the Sabbath began, without being able to trim them later. So there was nothing special about having their houses lit up on Friday evening, perhaps even for a shorter time than usual. On the contrary, to account for the ire of Roman critics, they must have been able to observe that Jewish houses were lit up more and longer than usual—with or without smoke—on Saturday evening. In other words, the many lamps at Troas, according to the final version of Acts, in a context of a prolonged vigil, coincide with what could be seen at Rome. The rabbinic tradition (*MBer* 8:5) retains a precept of lighting lamps on Saturday evening at the end of Sabbath, with a blessing mentioning the first day of Creation (Gen 1:3).

3. But what about the high windows or skylights of the earlier version? There is no point in mentioning them in a story that takes place at night, unless, perhaps, the group was waiting for the appearance of the dawn, which is mentioned in the narrative. Now the episode we are dealing with is precisely a night-long vigil, for Paul does not leave until morning, and it is not as if he is pressed for time, since it is at the end of a week's stay. The Essene-like Therapeutae of whom Philo writes practiced similar vigils, and at the moment of sunrise they would turn toward the east and address a prayer to heaven (*On the Contemplative Life* 64-90); Josephus's Essenes address their first prayer of the day to the rising sun (*J.W.* 2 §§128 and 148), a custom that has intrigued

commentators. Waiting for the sun, especially on the morning of the first day of the week (the day of the creation of light), recalls the prophecy of Zechariah to John the Baptist, whose task would be to proclaim "the visit of the rising sun from on high" (Luke 1:78), a remarkable image that carefully avoids any suggestion of veneration of the sun itself.

4. After the death of Jesus, on Friday 14 Nisan, the following Sunday (first day of the week), the day of the resurrection, was also that of the presentation of the first sheaf of the barley harvest, which, according to Leviticus 23:11, is made on "the day after the Sabbath." Paul, who has occasion to use the metaphor of the first-fruits (see 1 Cor 15:20), explains that the night is far advanced and the day is close (Rom 13:11ff.). These metaphors are not used by chance. In our episode, which is dated in reference to Passover but takes place on an ordinary weekend, the symbolism of the first day, repeated every week, prevails over the symbolic meanings of the annual Passover, and we are back to the same question that we have already seen regarding the breaking of the bread.

Now that we have cleared the ground, let us return to this puzzling episode, which could easily be dismissed as trivial or comic. It certainly has some strange aspects. Eutychus falls down in the middle of the night, yet is only restored alive to his friends and relatives at dawn, when Paul departs. No attempt is made to hide this improbability, which should be related to the rite cele-brated during the vigil. That consists of two principal phases: the breaking of the bread during the night and later on the arrival of the dawn. Onto this rite are superimposed Eutychus's fall, Paul's word announcing that he is alive, then *later on* his return at dawn. So the story of Eutychus ("Lucky") is a sort of eucharistic tale: an action expressing death (breaking of the bread, parallel to Eutychus's fall) coupled with a proclamation of life (the word over the bread and over Eutychus), then the rising sun (resurrec-tion, Eutychus's return, joy despite Paul's disappearance).

This structure is very close to what Paul has to say in 1 Corinthians 11:26: "Each time you eat this bread [. . .] you pro-claim the death of the Lord until he comes." There is a delay be-tween the death, proclaimed by a ritual act performed at night, and the return, marked by the light of a new day. This delay may be very long, like the return of the Messiah in an undefined future, or very brief, like the resurrection at dawn, which is about to break on the first day of the week, as befits a rite. On the other hand, the lamps shining in the midst of the night, in the final version of Acts, express at once death *and* resurrection. This is very close to the final statement in the account of the disciples of Emmaus that "they had recognized him in the breaking of the bread" (Luke 24:35).

Finally, the narrative, read with both "lamps" and "lights," may call to the reader's mind other vigils from Saturday to Sunday, whether annual or weekly, that begin with the lighting of lamps, continue through the night, with a celebration of the Eucharist after midnight, and end at daybreak.

The Caesarea story allows us to see that baptism has a prehistory, tied to a particular, rather closed environment, especially if it is not necessarily conferred "in the name of Jesus." The narrative of Troas, with its very realistic setting in which cosmic and human elements are combined with features that recall the Essenes, deals with the meaning of the "breaking of the bread." This rite expresses death and resurrection. Jesus is absent from the narrative and is not even named, but he is replaced by the young Eutychus, who dies and rises again. The rite, therefore, does not seem to be dependent on the person of Jesus, and so again there is a prehistory that we need to research.

Chapter Two

Baptism and Eucharist

The NT draws attention to a number of Jewish institutions, but without ever telling us how they worked. They are supposed to be known to the reader. The institutions that characterized the first Christian groups are mentioned in passing, and sometimes even give structural form to the narratives, but they are never clearly defined. We do not know from the NT, for instance, how baptism or the Eucharist was celebrated. What should we make of that? Were such institutions of only secondary importance, arising more or less haphazardly, whereas the essential thing for the first Christians was to proclaim the end time, a superior ethic, or the exceptional qualities of Jesus? Or rather, did the communities regard these institutions as of fundamental importance, but, perhaps for that very reason, did not publish an account of how they worked?

The former explanation is the one more usually adopted. Yet the previous chapter has brought out two facts: these institutions were apparently important and marginal Jewish groups preferred oral transmission and did not publish the laws proper to themselves. It is just these laws, however, that show through in the narratives. Starting from the hypothesis that baptism and the Eucharist are major institutions, we will pursue in this chapter a sort of detective inquiry, hunting for clues that may lead us to these cultural realities and enable us to understand them.

I. BAPTISM

A good place to start a search for the origins of Christian baptism is with John the Baptist. He is such a familiar figure to readers of the Gospels that it seems obvious that he is part of the picture. In reality, his position, so strongly emphasized in the prologue of the Fourth Gospel, is quite surprising. Just why is it necessary that John should prepare the way for Jesus? The method adopted here is to examine gestures and customs, and so we will not study John's biography as such but only what is relevant to the baptism that he preached. Then we shall look at Jesus and baptism, and finally at Christian baptism in the NT.

Modern research on the historical Jesus agrees that Jesus was baptized by John and that his mission properly speaking began from the moment when he became John's successor, though he eventually made some adjustments to his message and adopted a somewhat different style. In fact, things appear to have been rather more complex, for the Gospels also retain traces of another way of looking at Jesus and John, namely as parallel figures. On the one hand, Matthew 3:2 and 4:17 underline the continuity between them. They make the same proclamation: "Be converted, for the kingdom of heaven is very close." That suggests a development along the same lines. But there is also symmetry: Jesus and John are both among those who are not listened to, apparently for the same reason (Matt 11:16-19). According to Mark 6:14 and 8:28, Herod Antipas and the people think that Jesus is John returned from the dead; in Mark 9:11-13, the destiny of John, recognized as Elijah, is modeled on that of Jesus, Son of Man and Suffering Servant; in Mark 11:27ff. Jesus defends his authority in terms of that of John, or more exactly of his baptism. According to Luke 11:1-4, Jesus' disciples pray or wish to pray as John's do. The strongest parallel between the two is in John 3:22ff., where both are baptizing at the same time.

The differences between Jesus and John have led many to conclude that Jesus later parted company with John's practices, in particular his baptism. And yet there is the unmistakable fact that the first Christians, both Jews and Gentiles, were baptized (Acts 2:38, etc.). So the question that arises is simple, although commentators are divided over the answer: Is Christian baptism in continuity with John's, or is it a creation, or perhaps a restoration, made by the first communities?

1. JOHN'S BAPTISM

At the outset of a study of "John's baptism," it may be of some use to look first at the vocabulary. The Greek verb *baptizein* is an intensive form of *baptein;* the general sense is "to plunge," often with a nuance of "to drown, sink" or even "to cause to perish" (*J.W.* 4 §137). Whether used metaphorically or literally, the negative meaning predominates, even in Philo and Josephus, and is attested in the NT (Mark 10:38-39; Luke 12:50). There is no need to eliminate the negative or painful connotations of the term *baptizein;* since it is a rite of exchange (remission of sins), it must in some way be costly, like all biblical rituals.

The LXX uses the term, introducing the sense of ritual immersion (Sir 34:25; Jdt 12:7; cf. 2 Kgs 5:14) as distinct from the idea of "washing." Following this distinction and the normal meaning of the terms, "baptism" should designate a total immersion, but it does not necessarily mean that everywhere in the NT. The verb is used seventy-one times in the NT, mostly in the active or passive, which would imply that someone officiates. However, the title of "baptist" can in itself mean either one who baptizes another or one who practices ablutions; thus Justin speaks of a Jewish sect of "baptists" (*Dialogue with Tryphon* 80.4). In order to avoid confusion, other early Christian writings speak of "hemerobaptist" sects, a term that suggests daily ablutions; interestingly enough, it is sometimes applied to John the Baptist himself.

Behind the ambiguous terminology lie two questions. First, is John's baptism a single act to be performed once for all, as at first sight it seems to be, or are there further ablutions from time to time, as suggested by the fact that John settled in places with an abundant supply of water (Jordan; Aenon near Salim: John 3:23)? Second, what exactly was the role of the officiant? On the one hand, John appears to carry out a rite that is proper to himself and so linked with him personally. But according to Luke 3:21, Jesus is baptized after John has been arrested, so not by John himself. It is usually said that this is a secondary feature aimed at separating to the maximum Jesus' ministry from John's. Such a reply is not fully satisfactory, not only because of the continuity indicated above but especially because, according to Acts 18:25 (WT) and 19:3, John's baptism is found at Alexandria and Ephesus among the disciples of Jesus, well after both have left the scene.

The conclusion is that this baptism existed independently of whether or not John was there in person, and it could also be connected with Jesus. So it is not a gesture of personal affiliation with either John or Jesus but a rite of entry into a group, which still needs to be defined. In later Christian baptism, too, the identity of the officiant is not of primary importance. We have seen this in the case of Cornelius, where Peter simply orders him to be baptized; again, in Acts 22:16 Ananias tells Paul to "see that he gets baptized." So it appears that the role of an officiant is essentially that of a guarantor who invites or receives the newcomer.

We return to the origins of John's baptism. For the NT, especially for the Synoptic Gospels, John is the forerunner of Jesus. However, the question that John, from his prison, puts to Jesus (Matt 11:2-6 par.) shows that he is not sure whether Jesus is "the one who is to come." Besides, Jesus does not give a direct reply, or rather he declares that the judgment has arrived in reality, under the form of healings and forgiveness. John's hesitation is natural: in a context of imminent judgment, he had announced the coming of "one greater than himself," and it was not obvious that Jesus was that one. The proclaimed "baptism in spirit and fire" is a metaphor, with a suggestion of cataclysm. In fact, John announced the coming, not of a Messiah, but of the Lord, as implied by the allusions to Malachi 3:1ff.

The little dialogue in Matthew 3:13-15, in which John asks Jesus to baptize him, may well have been introduced by the evangelist, but it is instructive. Jesus replies that it is fitting to accomplish all justice. This is often understood as an echo of Isaiah 53:11, where the servant of the Lord, though personally innocent, takes on himself the sins of others in order to obtain their justification. Such an allusion is not impossible but is not proved beyond doubt. To take only the elements in the narrative, first Jesus refuses to let John become his disciple, thus answering a question that necessarily arises if the two really met, namely, why John did not follow Jesus, since at least some of his disciples did so. Next, it implies that even for Matthew, Jesus was a baptizer. Finally, Matthew 3:2 does not speak of "baptism for the forgiveness of sins" but only of conversion. In other words, baptism seals a relationship to God, whether the one baptized has been a sinner or not, for the important point is entry into the community that John is gathering by baptism in view of the end time. A similar remark can be made about the identification of Jesus by John as "lamb of God" (John 1:29ff.): it is a synthesis, with immediate reference to the Passover. There, too, some of John's disciples follow Jesus, though not John himself. Yet Jesus professes a great admiration for John, whom he identifies without hesitation.

Mark 1:4 says that John was "proclaiming a baptism of conversion for the forgiveness of sins." This implies several things. First, baptism is proclaimed by John, and not only administered. This proclamation has to do with the coming of the kingdom, since Luke 3:18 goes so far as to say that he "preached the gospel," which underlines his kinship with Jesus. Furthermore, between proclamation and baptism there is certainly an element of instruction and training. According to Luke 3:8 (cf. Matt 3:8), John first demands fruits worthy of repentance (or conversion), which suggests a certain process to be followed. That happens to be the aspect especially emphasized by Josephus: "Baptism appears agreeable to God if it is not used for the pardon of certain faults but for the purification of the body, after the soul has previously been entirely purified by justice" (*Ant.* 18 §117). In other words, baptism marks success in perseverance. Further, it involves entry into a group.

This group clearly regards itself as the true Israel, worthy to face the last times. Despite expressions which would have it that "the whole country of Judea and all the inhabitants of Jerusalem" came to John to be baptized in the Jordan (Mark 1:5 par.), there can have been no question of all the Jewish people, or even of an important proportion, and for a very simple reason: everything takes place without reference to the Temple, and in particular to the annual Day of Atonement (10 Tishri). This was a popular observance, to the point of providing a subsequent frame of interpretation for the redemptive work of Jesus: Hebrews 5:1f. explicitly understands Jesus as a high priest, with precise allusions to the ritual in Leviticus 16:6ff. It already offered an obvious setting in which to place a call to conversion. So, implicitly for John, then explicitly with Jesus and later Stephen, there is a polemic against the Temple and its function.

This important aspect allows us to make a comparison with the Essenes, as they are defined by the Qumran *Community Rule*. We have noted their insistence on separation from perverse folk and on departure for the desert with a view to recovering the practice of the "first ordinances" (chap. 1, §I.2); there is a sense of urgency. The observance prescribed is defined in terms of the Law of Moses and "what the prophets have revealed by the Holy Spirit." The community, and it alone, has the inspired interpretation; it alone is the Covenant (1 QS 5:8, 20; 6:15), and so the true Israel.

This kinship on a central aspect between John and the Essenes enables us to give a sense to contacts in details. Thus, according to 1 QS 2:25–3:12, the return of the sinner can be brought about only through a process of conversion duly certified, and not by a simple ritual of purification; but when the conditions have been fulfilled, baptism expresses the remission of sins (3:6-9). Similarly, 1 QS 5:13 stipulates: "Let the impious not enter into the water in order to touch the 'purity' of the holy." Baptism as a simple immersion has no automatic effect. This last passage introduces a new element: only baptism gives access to the "purity," by which is meant here the sacred meal of the community, consisting of bread and wine, which was restricted to the initiated. This meal is notoriously absent in the case of John, since it is even said explicitly that he "does not eat bread or drink wine" (Luke 7:33). We shall have occasion, however, to speak about it again with regard to the Eucharist.

Our findings so far go against a common view of John as essentially an isolated prophetic figure, whose baptism was some sort of dramatic gesture performed over all who presented themselves. On the contrary, John's baptism was a process of initiation into the body of those who regarded themselves as the people fit to meet God.

2. JOHN, JESUS, AND THEIR DISCIPLES

The position of John as forerunner has two facets: he announces Jesus and he is the model for Jesus. On the other hand, we have already pointed out a general parallel between John and Jesus.

John, for his part, does not survive his arrest (he is not raised from the dead), but throughout Luke–Acts he leaves a lasting trace by reason of his baptism. This difference of scope occurs again in John's proclamation, where he announces another baptism, in the Spirit (and fire, according to Matthew and Luke). This same Spirit features in the baptism and temptation of Jesus, but that too is an emblematic scene, for the Spirit is in fact manifested only later, at the occasion of baptism "in the name of Jesus" (Acts 2:38; 10:47; 19:6). So it seems that the real difference between John and Jesus is to be sought not in what they did but in what they left behind.

Thus, to evaluate the relationship between John and Jesus we need to look at their respective disciples. John's preaching is addressed to all and contains no special doctrine, except an exhortation to conversion (return to the Law), by way of proclaiming an imminent judgment. He has a wide influence and a reputation that makes him an object of fear on the part of the authorities (as Josephus makes clear). In truth, these features are largely common to both Jesus and John. In the latter case, however, the Gospels never show him organizing a group of disciples or even calling them personally. Some have concluded that John, as a charismatic leader, did not have disciples in the proper sense of the word and that only after his death did some groups claim to belong to him in order to distinguish themselves from the people or to resist the disciples of Jesus.

This conclusion is closely bound up with the identification of John as a prophet at the Jordan, his baptism being seen as a sort of extra piece of ornamentation. But it runs counter to a number of texts. Those cases already mentioned where "John's baptism" occurs in the absence of John himself, and without reference to his prophetic role, would indicate rather that baptism played an essential part and that there were disciples qualified to propagate it. In the Synoptics, John's disciples have a well-defined profile, distinct from the people in general: they fast (Mark 2:18-20 par.);

bury their master (Mark 6:29 par.); some follow Jesus; and according to Luke 11:1, John taught them how to pray. But above all, it is very difficult to see how disciples could have emerged after John's death if there had been none during his lifetime. This last is another form of the argument of Gamaliel (see Acts 5:36ff.), namely, that a vague movement surrounding a strong personality disappears with its founder if there is no successor or identifying structure to take over.

Was Jesus, then, John's designated successor? Not really, since, as we have seen in Matthew 11:2-6/Luke 7:18-23, John was not sure of his identity. The Fourth Gospel speaks clearly of John's disciples and relates those of Jesus to them according to two models. In John 1:37 they form a subdivision, since two of John's disciples follow Jesus, but in John 3:26ff. they are a parallel enterprise or even in competition. The only possible conclusion is that Jesus and John administered a baptism that had the same structure, as we shall see in connection with the disciples at Ephesus (Acts 19:1-7), and so their respective disciples had the same structure. The name "baptism of John" comes in part from the fact that John was earlier on the scene, but it also marks it off from the newly defined "baptism in the name of Jesus" that appears later with the Spirit (Acts 2:37ff.). Once again, the difference between the disciples is to be sought in what John and Jesus left behind. The Gospels, it is true, speak of large crowds coming to be baptized, but that is really an exaggeration linked to the interpretation of Jesus, like John, as a prophet. This point will emerge more clearly when we come to see "baptism" as a process and not as an isolated ritual act.

3. THE BAPTISM OF JESUS AND CHRISTIAN BAPTISM

To get a more precise idea of the place occupied by John, we now need to see if there is a link between the baptism received by Jesus and Christian baptism. At the beginning of the second century, Ignatius of Antioch and many after him explained that Jesus was baptized in order to purify the water by his passion (*Letter to the Ephesians* 18). Thus the water of baptism becomes a symbol of the redemptive death of Jesus, and in this way Jesus' baptism is related to Christian initiation. The divine manifestation, or theophany, that follows the baptism demonstrates that Jesus is Son of God according to the Spirit and so casts the light of the resurrection upon the Jesus of the ministry.

This theophany indicates a major transformation in what it means to be a disciple. For, insofar as it expresses Jesus' resurrection, the baptism that precedes it expresses his death. Now, if we follow what John actually proclaims, this baptism is meant to bring sinners back to fidelity to the Covenant, which at first sight is something quite different. The link between the two meanings is provided by the costly side of baptism, which is a test (whether by water, fire, or the Spirit). Here we note that according to Mark 1:5 par., those who come to John receive baptism "while confessing their sins." Baptism, at the end of a process of conversion, is also, therefore, an identifying mark of sin or of the sinner. The new meaning introduced by the baptism of Jesus takes this reality of sin to its ultimate significance: the sinner is likened to a dead person.

In this way the water of baptism takes on a new range of meanings. From being the essential element in purification (which supposes impurity and sin), it becomes the sign of death, which is possible only because there is something that follows, namely, resurrection and the Spirit. The symbolism of water can, therefore, include all mortal perils, the Deluge, the Red Sea, the storm on the lake, Jesus walking on the waters, the water and blood flowing from his side, etc. These remarks bring out the depth of meaning in Jesus' reply to John according to Matthew 3:15 ("Thus it is fitting for us to fulfill all justice"): by asking for baptism, Jesus enters into his mission. To sum up, the pair formed by Jesus' baptism and the theophany expresses the Christian kerygma (Jesus died and has been raised up) and at the same time recalls the mission entrusted to his disciples by the risen Christ ("Go, baptize . . ."; see Matt 28:19).

Paul's explanations now find their natural place, for example Romans 6:3-4: "Baptized into Christ Jesus, it is into his death that we have all been baptized; we have been buried with him into death . . . ." A further meaning can be seen in Jesus' baptism. He enters into the Law, since it is the restoration of the Law that John proclaims; then, this entry is transformed into victory over death.

This dimension enables us to understand the symbolism of baptism at the Jordan: it is entry into the Promised Land, that is, into eternal life.

So the baptism of Jesus has been broadly reinterpreted in terms of a later Christian perspective. From this conclusion we can retrace our steps through the tradition in order to get an idea of Jesus' activity as a baptizer. According to John 3:22–4:2, it was parallel to that of John, but with more success. There is no further mention of Jesus as a baptizer. Some authors conclude that Jesus at first adhered to John's enterprise, then was subsequently moved by the abandoned state of the populace to branch out on his own and proclaim mercy and free pardon, without necessity of previous conversion. But then, how do we account for the fact that Jesus' disciples quickly reinstated a practice that their Master had abandoned?

In fact, Jesus' activity as a baptist is at the heart of a sequence of episodes in these early chapters of John's Gospel, which hang together around the theme of baptism. As part of the complex narrative of the wedding at Cana, John 2:6ff. insists on the purification jars, in which the water is changed into wine. Jesus himself relates his "hour" to the filling of the jars, that is to say, he relates his death to purificatory (baptismal) water. The result is a wine superior to that served earlier, so the test of the "hour" is passed with flying colors.

Next, in the episode of the cleansing of the Temple (John 2:13ff.), Jesus, with an allusion to his death and resurrection, neutralizes the commercial system of sacrifices and so the whole *expiatory* cult. Then he declares to Nicodemus, "No one can enter the kingdom of God unless by being born of water and Spirit" (John 3:5). John 3:25 reports a discussion that John's disciples have with a Jew on the subject of purification; then they tell John that Jesus is having more success. The discussion is evidently about the meaning of baptism.

Finally, during the episode of the Samaritan woman Jesus speaks of "living water" (4:10), which is the technical term for the water of purification (as opposed to water that is stagnant or has been handled). As many have already pointed out, all these references form a homogeneous whole. Baptism as such is not mentioned in any of these passages, but it underlies them all, in the sense of providing a structure of meaning that brings very varied narrative elements together.

Thus there emerges a continuity of rite together with a change of meaning, but the latter is connected with the resurrection and not with any special features of Jesus as baptizer or healer. In the long run, it is impossible to make out a clear identity for the baptism administered by Jesus, which is neither the baptism of John nor later Christian baptism. In other words, whatever difference there may be between John's baptism and later Christian baptism does not come from anything created by Jesus during his ministry—he invented nothing and entered into a rite administered by another—but from a new meaning that is of later date. The texts discreetly reveal a continuity that is not in dispute. The Gospels reveal something similar in the case of the Eucharist, where also, materially speaking, Jesus invented nothing new but entered into an existing rite to which, however, a new meaning is given.

II. THE LAST SUPPER

If Jesus did not invent a new rite at the Last Supper, where did the rite come from? One answer commonly given supposes that the Last Supper was a Passover meal: the elements of bread and wine, which are consecrated and consumed in the Eucharist, were (and are) features of the Jewish Passover celebration. But the derivation of the Eucharist from the Passover celebration runs into serious difficulties. Put simply, was the Last Supper a Passover meal?

1. THE PROBLEM OF CHRONOLOGY

There is first a problem of chronology. The central difficulty can be stated very simply. All the gospel narratives agree in placing Jesus' death on a Friday, with a final meal on the previous Thursday evening. The Synoptic writers—Matthew (chap. 26), Mark (chap. 14) and Luke (chap. 22)—call this a Passover meal, and therefore celebrated on the evening of 14 Nisan (see Exod 12:6). According to this chronology, Jesus dies on the 15th. Now it is difficult to see how Jesus could have been tried and executed on the feast day itself. But in any case, for John (chap. 13), Jesus dies just before the beginning of Passover, thus on the 14th; further-more, John does not in any way suggest that the Last Supper was a Passover meal. So there is a contradiction or at least a lack of con-sistency. For completeness, let us add that Paul's account of Jesus' final meal (1 Cor 11:23-26) simply places it "on the night when he was handed over," without referring expressly to the Passover.

Three types of solution have tried to solve the difficulty. The first, implicitly adopted by the Church of Rome (which uses unleav-ened bread in the liturgy), essentially follows the Synoptics. What John has to say is then harmonized with them. The second solution, implicitly adopted by the Greek Church (which uses leavened bread in the liturgy), is to follow John, and so to suppose that Jesus put for-ward the Passover meal, knowing that he would be dead before the exact date on the following day. But that seems to be a rather odd thing to do, and in any case could not be guessed from the texts.

Alongside these traditional answers (which may even be ear-lier than the publication of the Gospels), there is a third type of solution, which is more elaborate and looks for a way of combin-ing both the others by suggesting that there were two Passover celebrations. The simplest is to suppose that because of the great number of pilgrims, the immolation of victims took place over two days, starting on 13 Nisan, especially for those from Galilee; that would explain why Jesus and his disciples ate the Passover on Thursday evening. However, there is no evidence for such a prac-tice, which would have involved all sorts of difficulties concern-ing leaven both for the Temple precincts and for the priests. In that case, it is tempting to imagine a controversy arising between the Pharisees and the Sadducees over what to do when Passover falls on a Sabbath: must the lambs be immolated on Thursday evening, and if so, should they be eaten immediately or left till Friday evening? Again, there is no trace of such a controversy, and in any case the supposed problem is artificial, since, it ap-pears, the lambs were slaughtered in the *afternoon* of the 14th, and so, in the case proposed, before the onset of the Sabbath.

A more subtle hypothesis would be to suppose disagreement about fixing the beginning of Nisan in that particular year, since it depends on witnessing the appearance of the new moon. Since a lunar month cannot have fewer than twenty-nine days or more than thirty, the uncertainty cannot be over more than one day, and for the year in question there may have been a double reckoning. However, the Pharisees and Sadducees all went to the same Temple, so it is not easy to see how two lots of public sacrifices would have been carried out, even if the priests had agreed to the duplication. In any case, there is no evidence of two official calculations existing side by side.

The most recent attempt to justify two celebrations of Passover calls on the solar calendar known from the *Book of Jubilees,* which was in use in circles connected with Qumran. According to this calendar, 1 Nisan is always a Wednesday, so the 14th is a Tuesday. On this basis Jesus celebrated the Passover and was arrested during the night of Tuesday-Wednesday (some early Christian writings support this chronology). So, it is suggested, the Synoptics followed this sectarian calendar, while John stuck to the official calendar of the Temple. The difficulty with this solution, however, is that the Synoptics agree with John that Jesus' Last Supper and arrest took place during the night of Thursday-Friday.

2. LAST SUPPER AND PASSOVER

Discussion of the calendar by itself seems to be getting us nowhere. Perhaps we should come at the question from another angle—the nature of the Last Supper.

Besides the explicit affirmation of the Synoptics that Jesus celebrated the Passover with his disciples on the night before he died, a number of incidental details in the narratives, not only in Matthew, Mark, and Luke but also in John, seem to support the view that the Last Supper was indeed a Passover meal: the time and the place of the meal; the few, chosen companions; and the fact that they recline on cushions (an exceptional gesture that was practiced at Passover).

Above all, the central features of the Last Supper, precisely those that have been handed down in the Christian Eucharist, seem to point to the Passover meal as their origin. In Matthew 26:26 and Mark 14:22, Jesus breaks the bread and pronounces the blessing *during* the meal; this gesture corresponds to the Passover rite, where, by way of exception the (unleavened) bread does not appear until after the first course. Furthermore, Jesus and his disciples drink wine during the meal, which was usual only on special (particularly family) occasions and on feasts. There is an obvious comparison with the Passover precept of drinking four cups of wine, which punctuate the festive meal; Luke 22:17-19 (AT), in fact, mentions two cups, one at the beginning and the other at the end. At the end of the meal, hymns were sung, no doubt all or part of the *Hallel* (Psalms 113–118), which is recited at Passover.

Perhaps the major argument for a Passover meal is the fact that Jesus announces his passion in words he pronounces over the bread and the wine. One of the characteristics of the paschal celebration is the obligation of interpreting certain parts of the meal, as suggested in Exodus 12:26ff., where the children question their parents about its unusual aspects.

In fact, however, the signs pointing to the identification of the Last Supper as a Passover meal are far from sure. A preliminary general caution: we should be careful not to assume that the Passover rite currently in use in rabbinic Judaism and prescribed in the traditional texts was practiced at the time of Jesus or at least was in general use then. Even a rapid comparison of the rabbinic rite with that laid down in Exodus 12:1-14 and still in use among the Samaritans reveals a number of differences. The most notable of these is the absence of the lamb itself, the central feature of the biblical rite. We shall return to this point later in this book.

If one element (the lamb) has disappeared from the rabbinic rite, another has come in, namely, the wine. Wine is not even mentioned in the passage from Exodus, but it occupies an important place in the rabbinic Passover rite, as it does in the Christian Eucharist. But there is more. In contrast with the rabbinic Passover, in which four cups of wine are drunk by all, Jesus blesses a single cup, which is then passed round, and so the amount drunk is strictly symbolic. In other words, if the Last Supper is placed within the setting of Passover, there is a serious discord: wine does not clearly play an intrinsic role in the Passover, whereas Jesus attaches major importance to it, even though only a small quantity is consumed.

Also non-biblical but part of the rabbinic Passover, as of the Synoptic and Pauline narratives of the Last Supper, is the blessing over bread during or at the beginning of the meal. In fact, in Deuteronomy 8:10 the only blessing prescribed is one said after having eaten and being filled, and so at the end of a meal. However, in the name of the general rule forbidding enjoyment of any good thing of this world without first blessing the Creator, the rabbinic tradition prescribes a blessing before tasting anything at all and gives various formulas for this purpose, according to the different kinds of natural produce (fruit, vegetables, cereals, etc.; meat, fish, dairy products, etc.). But from this emerges the exceptional position of bread and wine: they are produced by human work and not simply by nature, and each has a special blessing attached to it, as distinct from wheat and grapes, which are included in the general categories of produce of the soil and fruit.

If the Last Supper was in fact a Passover meal, it is surprising that the elements chosen by Jesus to comment on, the bread and wine, do not appear to be the most appropriate signs. Why not speak of the bitter herbs on the eve of his passion? Why does he identify himself with the bread and not with the paschal lamb, as in 1 Corinthians 5:7ff. and John 1:29, etc.? Why comment on the wine, which is a secondary element? And if the bread is important, the comparison with the manna (John 6:26ff.) is much clearer and has a richer meaning than the unleavened bread. In other words, bread and wine already have a sufficiently strong identity to require that they be taken as the signs conveying the meaning of Jesus' death. That is not so obvious in the Passover meal. Once again, the bread and the wine stand out.

3. LOOKING FOR A MEANING

In order to get any further, we need to go back to the texts and analyze them, concentrating on the various stages of the meal itself. To lighten the presentation, we shall omit the first part of the meal concerning the betrayal (or the "handing over") introduced in Matthew 26:21 and Mark 14:18 by the expression "while they were eating," which is picked up again at the beginning of the passage cited here. (Luke has a different organization; here too there are two forms of his narrative, one given by the WT, the other by the AT):

Matt 26	Mark 14	Luke 22 WT	1 Cor 11
Cf. v. 29	Cf. v. 25	(15) And he said to them: I have desired with a (great) desire to eat this Passover with you before suffering. (16) For I tell you that I will not eat it again until it is fulfilled in the kingdom of God. (17) Then taking a cup, he gave thanks and said: Take and share (it) among you. (18) For I tell you, I will not drink henceforth of the produce of the vine until the kingdom of God has come.	
Cf. v. 29	Cf. v. 25		
			(23) The Lord Jesus, the night he was handed over,
(26) Now, while they were eating, Jesus, taking bread and blessing broke (it) and giving (it) to his disciples, said: Take, eat, this is my body	(22) And while they were eating, taking bread, blessing, he broke (it) and gave (it) to them and said: Take, this is my body.	(19) And taking bread, he gave thanks, he broke (it) and gave (it) to them, saying: This is my body, given for you.	took bread, (24) and, giving thanks broke (it) and said: This is my body, for you.
		Do this in memory of me.	Do this in memory of me.
(27) And taking a cup	(23) And taking a cup,	(20) And the cup likewise after the meal,	(25) And likewise the cup after the meal,
and giving thanks he gave (it) to them, saying: Drink of it all, (28) For this is my *Covenant blood*,	giving thanks he gave (it) to them, and they all drank it. (24) And he said: This is my *Covenant blood*	*[Added by AT]* saying: This cup (is) *the new Covenant* in my blood,	saying: This cup is *the new Covenant* in my blood.
which is shed for many, in remission of sins.	which is shed for many.	which is shed for you.	
			Table continued on following page.

Matt 26	Mark 14	Luke 22 WT	1 Cor 11
		This, do it, each time that you drink, in memory of me. (26) For, each time that you eat this bread and that you drink this cup, you will announce the death of the Lord,	
(29) Now I tell you, from now on I will not drink of this produce of the vine until the day when I drink it with you, new, in the kingdom of my Father.	(25) Amen I tell you that I will no longer drink of this produce of the vine until the day when I drink it with you, new, in the kingdom of God.	Cf. v. 18.	until he has come.

Without losing sight of the context, we shall make a comparative study of these texts, first in general, then in more detail.

1. Whatever the complexities of the calendar, the literary context of Matthew, Mark, and Luke is that of Passover. This feast traditionally has two dimensions: the commemoration of the deliverance from Egypt (Exod 12–13) and the celebration of the entry into the Promised Land (at Gilgal: Josh 5:10ff.). This second Passover has a notable feature: it corresponds to the cessation of the manna, as the Israelites then begin to eat the produce of the land, beginning with unleavened bread. In the Gospel accounts of the Last Supper, there are no allusions to the Exodus, but there are very clear references to the Promised Land, expressed in terms of the kingdom of God: Jesus announces a future celebration in the kingdom. This is particularly clear in Luke 22:15-18, with explicit references to the lamb and the wine. The same distance between the present and an undefined future is indicated also in Matthew 26:29 and Mark 14:25, but only in regard to "the produce of the vine." The episode takes place not simply in Judea but in Jerusalem, where Jesus has insisted on coming. However, this is not a true arrival but a departure (a failed arrival). There is a messianic dimension, seen clearly in the tradition that the Messiah will return one night of Passover.

2. Allusions to the Covenant and to blood (Matt 26:29 par.) strike a note that does not appear to be directly related to Passover, since there is no connection with the lamb, not even with the blood rite of Exodus 12:22ff. On the other hand, the "Covenant blood" of Matthew and Mark alludes to the sacrifice that seals the revelation at Sinai (Exod 24:8), and the "new Covenant" of 1 Corinthians (and Luke AT) refers to Jeremiah 31:31. Comparison with sectarian documents provides a more precise context. For *Jubilees* 29:7, the feast of the Covenant is Pentecost, which always falls on a Sunday, the fifteenth day of the third month; it is also the feast of the first-fruits. According to this text, the Covenant as such is not attached to Moses; it begins with Noah (*Jub* 6:17) and continues with Abraham (*Jub* 14:1ff.; see Gen 15:7ff.). With Moses, therefore, the *same* Covenant is renewed, but now with a real nation (see 1 QS 3:4bis).

3. As a result of these observations, we can bring together the two expressions "blood of the Covenant" and "new Covenant." In both cases, it is the same Covenant being renewed, without abandoning an earlier one, first by Moses, then by all who commit themselves to returning to his Law. There is even a sort of cycle: the people are fickle, but there is always a faithful remnant led by divinely inspired guides, whom the *Damascus Document* (2:11-12) calls the "anointed of his Holy Spirit." So the sect, which is none other than the "remnant," regards itself as the true Israel, that is, as the concrete expression of the Covenant, and to enter the community is to enter the Covenant, as we shall see (chap. 6, §II). Thus Pentecost, as feast of the Covenant, has a twofold dimension: the admission of newcomers and liturgical renewal of the Covenant, with appropriate ablutions. Obviously, this perspective gives a meaning that is both very simple and very central to the Pentecost of Acts 2, which concludes with numerous baptisms.

4. In this perspective of the ancient feast of Pentecost, we can give a meaning to the characteristic elements of bread and wine at the Last Supper and in the Christian Eucharist. We have seen that they do not fit well into the setting of Passover. By contrast, Pentecost is also the feast of first-fruits, and according to Leviticus 23:17, those to be presented first are none other than the first-fruits

of ordinary *(leavened)* bread. It is to be noted that this is not the produce of the earth in a raw state, such as wheat, but a prepared food. Besides this basic feature of the feast properly so called, other Essene texts (11 QT 18-22 and 43; 4 QMMT A) indicate a rhythm of fifty-day periods, so little pentecosts always falling on a Sunday, when new wine (must), then oil—once again, prepared produce—are offered. Thus the *first-fruits* of bread and wine are related to the cycle of Pentecost, with an eschatological significance that is central: eating the fruits of the new year, which represent the new world, new creation, etc.

But the link with Pentecost and the Covenant is not limited to the dates imposed by the solar calendar. The gesture of offering and eating first-fruits can be made at any time, as we see in the appendix to the Qumran *Community Rule* (or *Rule of the Congregation*): the messianic meal described in 1 QSa 2:11-22, with the two messiahs (son of Aaron and son of David) and the rest of the people in tribes, shows the priest (messiah son of Aaron) opening the meal with a blessing of the first-fruits of bread and wine. More interesting still, this rite is already to be observed in a minor form at every meal where there are at least ten people present, as in 1 QS 6:4-5; Josephus says simply twice a day, after purification (*J.W.* 2 §133ff.).

Comparison with the Last Supper of Jesus becomes easy when one recalls that there the rite concerns a single loaf and a single cup, and not all the bread provided and the whole jug of wine or the cups of all those present. It is a question then of only a small but venerated part of the foodstuff, which aptly expresses a setting apart of first-fruits. Later Christian tradition knows two types of ritual meals: the *agapē,* or Lord's Supper, during which each person eats normally, and the *Eucharist,* with a characteristic thanksgiving and only symbolic consumption. According to the sources, these two forms were originally combined but later separated. The witness of 1 Corinthians 11 and the accounts of the Last Supper attest the earlier state: a symbolic meal and an ordinary meal, the symbolic part being a sign of first-fruits. In this way it is easy to see how the Last Supper is told in a way that suggests a *habitual* meal taken by Jesus and his disciples and distinct from Passover.

5. However, in the present state of the texts, everything has been inserted into a setting that is paschal and so messianic. Once again the Essene texts referred to give us a way of approaching this. The solemn renewal of the Covenant has a priestly dimension (1 QSb 3:26, cf. Si 54:25); the meal described, taken as it is in the present age, is presided over by a priest, who makes an eschatological sign of first-fruits. But the ultimate reality hoped for is described by Isaiah 11:1ff.: it is the son of David who will intervene at the end, when Israel will be saved and the impious will be slain (1 QSb 5:20ff.; 4 QPB 3-4; 4 QFl 1:11-13). This is a post-priestly messianism, whose imagery is warlike but has no particular political relevance.

We can thus make a clear distinction, at least in theory, between Zealots and Essenes. The former propose immediate political action, in anticipation of the last times; but it is not a true messianism, for the simple reason that the leaders who emerge have no claim to Davidic descent. By contrast, the Essenes have in view two phases that are quite distinct: the present time, with a priestly ideal and an eschatological ritual, and the future time, in a reality that lies beyond any rite. Typically, according to *J.W.* 2 §142, when newcomers are admitted, they must undertake to abstain from Zealot activism.

6. These aspects of messianism throw light on the Last Supper. In fact, the reference to Passover is twofold: the Passover that was being celebrated at the time, corresponding to the death of Jesus, and a future Passover, corresponding to the coming of the kingdom—in other words, the failure of a more or less overt messianism ending in Jerusalem and the announcement of a final messianism, duly transformed. Between the two, the rite of bread and wine, with its connotations of Pentecost, is an eschatological sign in the present time (which other NT passages express as a symbolic participation in a heavenly liturgy). Pentecost and its associated signs, along with the Spirit, correspond to the keeping of the Covenant, that is, to the time of the Church. We are dealing with a rite, with an act, that is in some way incomplete, since it needs to be repeated, corresponding to an eschatology that is in the course of being realized. The final reality, however, is represented by Passover. This interpretation

enables us to understand the Synoptic Gospel accounts as resulting from the insertion of two items into the actual Passover of Jesus: the eschatological sign of the bread and wine and a comment on the messianic rendezvous to come. This is particularly clear in Matthew and Mark; in Luke the two insertions are closer together, as the present and future Passovers come at the beginning and the breaking of the bread only afterward.

7. So behind the account of the Last Supper there is indeed a liturgical tradition that is independent of Passover. It is none other than a sort of community meal in which the significant elements are bread and wine. This is not a feast but only the first stage of a complete meal (which may or may not be festive), since the share that each receives is minimal and would not normally be sufficient as food. The central meaning that it symbolizes is connected with Pentecost, signifying both the renewal of the Covenant (Sinai) and an anticipation of the kingdom (first-fruits). It has a weekly expression, linked to the night between Sabbath and the first day of the week (watching for the dawn). It may also have a daily expression, judging from the episode of the pilgrims from Emmaus, from the tradition in 1 Corinthians 11, where the eve of Jesus' death could be any day at all, and even from the fact that the foodstuffs taken are extremely common. This layout, which is in general agreement with Essene customs, is found in the whole of later Christian tradition with remarkable regularity.

8. Finally, the NT and some related texts place especial emphasis on the *breaking* of the bread before its consumption. Here it is clearly more than a simple utilitarian act; it is a significant gesture, a rite, practiced by Jesus with his disciples. The rite was in itself capable of more than one signification, which was expressed in an accompanying prayer of blessing or thanksgiving. These meanings are often articulated in a negative moment followed by a positive moment. One that is expressed or alluded to in several places (Mark 6:30-44; *Did.* 9:4) is the scattering, then the eschatological ingathering of God's people—Israel, then the Church.

According to Paul, Jesus at the Last Supper, as he blessed, broke, and distributed the bread, then blessed and passed the cup, said: "Do this in memory of me" (1 Cor 11:24). The emphasis here is not on the "Do this"— they were doing it anyway—but on "in memory of me." What they were already in the habit of doing they were thenceforth to do in memory of Jesus. So for Paul, whenever we eat this bread and drink this cup, we are proclaiming the death of the Lord until he comes (1 Cor 11:26): the familiar rite now symbolizes the negative moment of Jesus' death followed by the positive moment of his awaited return. Luke, as we have seen, expresses rather a realized eschatology when he recounts how the two disciples on the journey to Emmaus "had recognized him in the breaking of bread" (Luke 24:35; see chap. 1, §II.2).

The rite itself still plays an integral part in all the Christian liturgical traditions. Its meaning has, however, been somewhat lost sight of, or rather it has been transferred to the entire eucharistic action (and, in the Roman tradition since the Middle Ages, especially to the twofold consecration of the elements).

III. CONCLUSIONS

Christianity was born in a well-defined environment that was socially and politically marginal. When Jesus passed through this environment, it was certainly an event of the first importance, but always within the setting and the values of this environment, as we are beginning to see clearly. So we can understand that whether he was accepted or rejected, it was as an internal phenomenon, not something exotic. Furthermore, reinterpretations came about through disruptions. John announced a cataclysm, and a cataclysm did indeed occur, but not in the way expected. The Gospels typically show the death of Jesus, then the first manifestations of the Spirit, as cosmic disturbances. In parallel to this, the apostles are shown as totally unable to cope, in the act of betrayal, denial, or flight. It is indeed a cataclysm, a sort of return to primeval chaos. Thus it is understandable that when the disciples start off again, they hold on to the elements that had formed their identity and their companionship with Jesus, namely, the ritual gestures to which they were accustomed "since the baptism of John" (Acts 1:22).

The two scenes that served to get us under way—Peter's visit to Cornelius and the night at Troas—featured baptism and the breaking of the bread. Further study of baptism in the NT and the Last Supper has been greatly helped by parallel texts of Essene origin. We are obviously dealing with the same sort of Jewish culture, which is very different from the kind of Judaism that Philo and Josephus set out to present in published form. All the same, we have to take due account of a major difference. The Essenes constitute a very traditional reform movement, strictly internal to Judaism and condemning all those who do not belong to it. On the other hand, among Jesus' disciples there appears, at a particular moment, an opening up to the Gentiles. But Jesus himself took on the yoke of the Law through the baptism of John and did not look beyond the "lost sheep of the house of Israel."

How do we account for this revolutionary change? Should we look to Galilee for the answer?

Chapter Three

Jewish Galilee

Many modern studies on Christian origins start from the more or less explicit idea that since Galilee was distant from Jerusalem, it was easier there to be free of the Law and the oversight of the Temple. The biblical expression "Galilee of the nations" (Isa 8:23 LXX, quoted by Matt 4:15) has become a cliché readily lending itself to an impression of Galilee as a region where (not very orthodox) Jews rubbed shoulders with Gentiles. In just such an environment, one might imagine, a Galilean teacher and/or his followers could already be disposed to a greater openness toward the Gentile world and even believe themselves called to "go to the Gentiles." The trouble is, however, that such an impression is not at all supported by the way the Book of Acts depicts the opening to the Gentiles; it also runs counter to the true picture of Jewish Galilee that emerges from a close study of the sources. Furthermore, how is it that Galilee should be an essential point of reference not only for the Gospels but also for Flavius Josephus and for the rabbinic tradition? That is hardly to be expected of a remote and marginal province whose Jewish identity is doubtful. Let us begin to look more closely.

Galilee does not play any appreciable role in the OT. In the NT, the Galilee in which Jesus moves is rural, without any mention of the capital cities of Sepphoris or Tiberias but reflecting a high degree of religious motivation: expectations, debates, and conflicts within groups of various tendencies. Since the later development of Christianity, as seen in Acts, is eminently urban

(Caesarea, Antioch, Corinth, Ephesus, Rome), these rural beginnings are unlikely to have been a pure creation of the first communities. So we are dealing here with a fact. What were the nature and origin of this Jewish environment without obvious roots in the Bible, distant from the big centers, and, what is more, separated from Jerusalem by hostile Samaria?

Josephus, anxious to establish his right to speak in the name of his people, drew up his autobiography *(Life)* around A.D. 90. The curious thing is that he devotes the greater part of this work to going over once again his old campaigns in Galilee during the uprising of 66. He is obviously pleading a case, but, contrary to his first account in *The Jewish War,* he entirely omits from this second version any direct engagement of importance against the Romans and concentrates almost entirely on divisions among the Jews. No doubt something of this is due to his position as an imperial freedman defending imperial policy, but the result is that, viewed from Rome, the events that he retells seem to be of strictly local interest in terms of their political and social consequences. About the same time, when describing in the *Jewish Antiquities* the main "philosophies" within Judaism, he has to add to the famous triad of Pharisees-Sadducees-Essenes a fourth tendency, that of the Galilean Zealots, whose origins can be traced back to the beginning of the Roman occupation. What made him dignify this movement in such a way, since just before he fiercely criticized the Zealots as responsible for the conflicts that brought about the downfall of Jerusalem? There seem to have been some strictly Jewish reasons that obliged him even at Rome to give serious attention to far-off Galilee and the Galileans more than twenty years after the events.

In a quite different context, the Mishnah, the fundamental collection of rabbinic Judaism, also comes from Galilee. It was edited about A.D. 220 by Rabbi Judah the Prince (or Patriarch), and despite numerous reminiscences of Jerusalem and the Temple, its general atmosphere is rural. Shortly afterward, the Mishnah was transferred to Babylonia, where it was adopted. However, it did not at this time spread into the Mediterranean basin, even though the contemporary Severan dynasty at Rome was rather favorable to the Jews, and the emperor Caracalla had granted Roman citizenship to all free subjects of the empire, including the Jews (A.D. 212). Later generations of commentators produced two collections, known as the Jerusalem Talmud (originating in fact in Galilee) and the Babylonian Talmud, which are culturally twins. However, the Mishnah presents itself as the work of schools founded by refugees from Judea after the defeat of Bar Kokhba, the Romanization of Jerusalem (Aelia), and the expulsion of the Jews from Judea. What were the nature and origin of this Galilean Judaism? And why did it turn in the direction of Babylonia? In any case, the entire phenomenon is quite marginal to the Roman world.

So we need to define the typical features of Jewish Galilee. What can we know from Josephus and from the rabbinic literature?

I. GALILEE UNTIL HEROD

Geographically, the term "Galilee," meaning something round and suggesting "rolls" or "waves," designates strictly the region of rolling hills north of the Plain of Esdraelon and west of the Jordan (Upper Galilee). It is a small, though fertile, rural province, corresponding approximately to the territory assigned in the Bible to the four tribes of Asher, Issachar, Naphtali, and Zebulun. These tribes formed part of the post-Solomonic kingdom of Israel. The original meaning of the expression "Galilee of the nations" (or: "of the Gentiles") is simply "ring of the nations," with an overtone of enemy encirclement; this little region was exposed and lacking in fortified towns. In the finale of Matthew 28:16ff., the risen Christ summons his disciples to Galilee to send them out to all nations, so that Galilee appears to be the gateway to the Gentiles. This is, however, a transformation of Galilee analogous to the resurrection of Jesus himself.

1. AFTER THE EXILE

At the time of the Maccabean uprising, we hear of Jews in Galilee (1 Macc 5:14ff.). Under persecution, they appealed to Judas and his brothers for help, declaring that they were the victims of a coalition bringing together Ptolemais, Tyre, Sidon, and all Galilee (which corresponds well to the "ring of the nations"). Simon led an expedition to bring them to Jerusalem. This event took place between 167 and 160 B.C. It was a question, at most, of a thinly spread minority, without a stronghold of their own, in contrast to other regions. These scattered folk do not seem to have been migrants from Judea, and it is arbitrary to regard them as direct descendants of ancient Israelites, whose natural ties would in that case have been with Samaria. So who were they and where did they come from?

The only notable event to which this precarious settlement of Jews in Galilee can be attached is the charter granted to Jerusalem by the Seleucid king Antiochus III around 200 B.C. The circumstances were as follows. After a century of domination of Palestine and Phoenicia by the Ptolemies of Egypt, Antiochus had some difficulty in integrating these regions into his own kingdom, but the inhabitants of Judea and the Jews in general were on his side. As a reward he granted a charter that recognized the status of Jerusalem. But it also allowed "all those who form part of the Jewish people" to live according to their own national laws. This latter provision obviously applied to more than just Judea. In fact, there had long been a large Jewish population throughout Babylonia (Mesopotamia) and the Seleucid empire. In addition, Antiochus did not hesitate to use Jews as civilian colonists in distant parts of his empire to stabilize disputed border areas. If they were faithful to their ancestral laws, these settlers could not enlist in any army because of the Sabbath but would peacefully occupy the land and so ensure maximum security.

It is logical to suppose that as a consequence of the charter, Jewish settlers from various parts of the Seleucid empire, whether sent expressly or coming as volunteers, arrived in fertile Galilee. It is also reasonable to suppose that the traffic entailed by pilgrimages and the dispatch of offerings for the Temple led to the creation of halts on the land route from Mesopotamia, which passed through Damascus and Scythopolis (Beth-Shean). These suppositions get some support from the results of archaeological surveys in Galilee. These show, for the Hellenistic period, a small population before the second century and then a large-scale rural settlement, but scattered and without much in the way of towns. It is a sign that Antiochus III's policy was working. Despite the rescue operation of the Galilean Jews that we saw above, the social and political attachment of Galilee to Judea remained rather vague until the reorganization of the whole region by the Romans after 64 B.C. On the other hand, the links with Babylonia remained strong and were constantly reinforced by pilgrimages and other contacts.

What stands out from all this is the exceptional position of the Jews of Galilee. They had no identifiable connection with the ancient northern kingdom (Israel) or with the Samaritans; they did not belong to the political entity of Judea; and despite Josephus's story about the Itureans, they were not the result of the forced circumcision of local tribes. We shall see, however, that they had a cultural identity that was very marked.

2. AROUND HEROD THE GREAT

The young Herod began his military and political career in Galilee. He was the son of a certain Antipater, who had risen to power under the last of the Hasmonean kings of Judea. In reality, of course, Judea, like its neighbors, had already passed under Roman dominance. Antipater was not by ancestry a Jew but an Idumean who had accepted circumcision; Herod was never able to shake off the imputation of being, at best, a "half-Jew." Among other feats that he accomplished in Galilee, he crushed a certain Ezekias and his band of "brigands," who were at large on the Syrian border. But a trial followed before the Sanhedrin at Jerusalem, and Herod was prosecuted by Pharisees. This was the beginning of a struggle between Herod and the Pharisees that was to last throughout his reign. In fact, this Ezekias was not simply a bandit; he can be regarded as the ancestor of the militant religious nationalists whom Josephus represents as a "fourth philosophy." The "brigands" were therefore anti-Roman Jews to whom the Pharisees of the time were favorable. They were centered in Galilee.

In 40 B.C. Herod had himself appointed king of Judea by the Roman senate. He obtained this promotion thanks to a war against the Parthians, the great power in the East, in which Rome needed local allies. In the following year Herod, with the support of the Romans, landed at Ptolemais in order to conquer Judea. Josephus affirms that the whole of Galilee rapidly rallied to him "with some exceptions" and that he made his way to Jerusalem with ever-growing forces. Nevertheless, he was obliged to go back to Galilee in order to consolidate his hold on the province. He entered Sepphoris without striking a blow but had to commit considerable forces in a difficult struggle against "brigands living in caves."

Josephus tells how, after the main force of the enemy had been defeated, an assault was made on the caves where the last re-sisters held out. They were in the cliffs of Arbela, above Magdala on the shore of the Lake (*Ant.* 14 §§421ff.). A notable incident: on the point of being captured, one old man (or "elder") refused to give himself up and preferred to kill his wife and seven children and throw himself over the edge. Herod was on the spot and held out his hand in a sign of pardon, but the other, before jumping off, took time to shout abuse at him because of his foreign origins. So these were not brigands who pillaged for gain; indeed, the episode resembles those, a century later, of the prisoners at Jotap-ata and even the collective suicides at Gamala and Massada. It seems that these brigands were akin to the Ezekias who had been vanquished by Herod ten years previously: his outstretched hand expresses the hope of winning not only victory but also recogni-tion. In any case, it is noteworthy that Herod sought the backing of Galileans, as Josephus himself was to do in somewhat similar circumstances.

Josephus tells later (*Ant.* 17 §§23ff.) how, at a period which is not well defined but probably soon after the beginning of his reign, Herod wanted protection for his northeastern border from raiders, probably Arab or Nabatean Bedouins operating out of Trachonitis. In order to set up a buffer zone in Batanea (Golan), the king created a peaceful Jewish settlement that could protect the pilgrimage route as well as the district. He installed a group of Babylonian Jews who were already in Syria and were well re-garded by the Romans. He gave them lands to break in and ex-empted them from taxes. Their leader, called Zamaris, built a town, Bathyra, and several strongholds. He summoned from everywhere "people faithful to the Jewish customs." Tax-free status and a remote situation were very attractive, especially for folk who had a high degree of religious motivation but were not interested in furthering political ambition. Herod's choice of Babylonian Jews who were not interested in politics was certainly clever, especially in view of the nearby Galileans on the other shore of the Lake who had resisted him; they had also come from Babylon in earlier migrations.

When Herod died, in 4 B.C., the situation once again became confused, with succession disputes around Archelaus, abuse of power by the Roman army, and various uprisings, especially on the occasion of the pilgrimages to Jerusalem at Passover and Pentecost. The religious factor counted for much in these revolts. The troubles were put down by Varus, governor of Syria. He showed clemency toward Jerusalem but was pitiless with regard to the "brigands."

In Galilee, Sepphoris was at the center of a rebellion led by Judas of Gamala, who sought to profit from the weakness of Jerusalem and take over the government. The revolt was put down and the town destroyed by Varus's son (*Ant.* 17 §289). This Judas is none other than Judas "the Galilean," the founder *together with a Pharisee* of the "madness" that Josephus is constrained to call a "fourth party" (*Ant.* 18 §§4f.). Judas is represented as the "son of Ezekias," who was, of course, the one whom Herod had beaten more than forty years previously. Obviously Judas was his successor rather than his own son: the dates are too far apart and no genealogy is given, so the meaning here has to be that they are of the same "breed."

At the time of the fiscal census under Quirinius in A.D. 6, Judas was sufficiently influential to incite widespread resistance to Roman power (and taxes) throughout Judea. Hence the label "the Galilean," which was certainly given by others and supposes appreciable influence outside Galilee itself; since it could be applied to a native of the Golan rather than of Galilee, its connotation, in this context, is not primarily geographical. Such influence did not come about overnight, and it was against this deeply anti-Roman party that Varus moved most severely. So Jewish Galilee was strengthened under Herod, to the point of taking on a national importance that will only grow subsequently. Along with this we need to place the fact that the Pharisees never wanted to give their allegiance to Herod, who feared and persecuted them (see *Ant.* 17 §§41ff.). Even though it was only a rural province without great economic or strategic importance, Herod's maneuvers and the social instability after his death show both the difficulty and the importance of being in control of Galilee.

II. HILLEL AND GALILEE

The previous section, showing Herod's behavior with regard to Galilee and the Pharisees, provides a setting for the appearance of Hillel the Elder and a means of evaluating the rabbinic sources that mention him. Hillel is one of the great founding figures of normative Judaism and the first to whom tradition accords the title of patriarch. It is also with him that rabbinic tradition begins to notice controversies, which has puzzled later commentators; so he brings together several distinct currents. Hillel came from Babylonia and lived at the time of Herod, but little more can be said with certitude about him.

1. A DISTANT ENTHRONEMENT

Josephus, who has eyes only for what counts socially, ignores Hillel but mentions Shemaya and Abtalion, who immediately precede Hillel and Shammai in the list of transmitters of the tradition given in the Mishnah (*MAb* 1:10ff.). The narrative of Hillel's installation as patriarch is given only by the rabbinic sources, and its main interest lies in the evidence it provides of a major discontinuity between him and his immediate predecessors. The event is reported in several similar forms; the longest and best-documented version is in the Jerusalem Talmud (*YPes* 6:1 p. 33a). It is set in Bathyra, the Jewish settlement established by Herod in the Golan.

It happened one day that 14 Nisan fell on a Sabbath, and (the Elders) did not know if the Passover sacrifice took precedence over the Sabbath or not. They said: "There is here a certain Babylonian whose name is Hillel, who has studied with Shemaya

*and Abtalion. He will know if the Passover sacrifice takes prece-
dence over the Sabbath"—"Can he be of any use!?" They sent
for him. They said to him: "Have you ever heard if, when 14
Nisan falls on a Sabbath, it takes precedence over it or not?"*

Hillel tries to prove the point by various arguments based
above all on the Bible and using his rules of interpretation, but the
others refuse his reasons or disprove them, then conclude: *"There
is nothing to get from this Babylonian!"*

*Although he had stayed to give them explanations all day
long, they did not accept him until he said to them: "Woe is me!
That is what I received from Shemaya and Abtalion." When they
heard that, they rose and designated him as patriarch.*

The examination that Hillel undergoes is remarkable on
more than one score:

a) The entity that questions Hillel has the power to appoint
him as "patriarch," at least in the sense of head of a school. It is in
no way said that this entity is a sanhedrin; it is only the "Elders of
Bathyra," who are hardly mentioned elsewhere but have strong
ties with Babylonia.

b) The masters who are mentioned, Shemaya and Abtalion,
are the authorities recognized by all, but they are absent and have
not been replaced.

c) The profile of the candidate who is sought is quite particular: a Babylonian who has frequented Pharisee masters in Judea.
However, in the account in question, some challenge the Babylonian as such. So there is a problem of unifying different currents.

d) The context of the question asked is not academic but indicates a concrete emergency that cannot be met either by a firm tradition or by an authority on the spot capable of giving a decision.
The Mishnah, at least in the form in which it was edited two centuries later, is unknown, but there is no tribunal or teacher vested
with the necessary authority because of the break in continuity.

e) The question itself is odd, for according to the normal
lunar calendar, Passover falls on a Sabbath on average every
seven years. It is somewhat improbable that the entire assembly

capable of promoting Hillel should have forgotten a point of custom so general and so simple.

The way this episode is put together presents a thick bundle of problems. Hillel's enthronement has shown a break in continuity between Shemaya and Abtalion and their successors, in an atmosphere of crisis, and we must suspect that these teachers were eliminated along with the rest of the Sanhedrin by Herod. Josephus is very hard to pin down on the question of whether Herod acted against the Sanhedrin as soon as he came to power. His maneuverings do, however, give us one piece of useful information: he has difficulty in placing Shemaya (or Samaias/Sameas) and Abtalion (or Pollion) in a historical context and does not speak of them in the *Jewish War* (see *Ant.* 14 §§172ff.; 15 §§3-4; §370). He knows, however, or rather he has learned, that they are remembered as important by the Pharisees, so even though they disappeared under Herod, their reputation in certain circles has earned them a lasting influence. He attempts to free Herod from blame by suggesting that his purges took place before Shemaya and Abtalion left the scene.

It is possible, however, to explain the discontinuity before Hillel in another way. The traditional succession from Shemaya and Abtalion to Hillel (and Shammai, a different form of the name Shemaya) may be nothing more than a simple literary device. In that case, the narrative of Hillel's installation with the anachronistic title of patriarch would combine the origin in Babylonia, represented by the colony at Bathyra and Hillel, with the teaching of Pharisees at Jerusalem, represented by Shemaya and Abtalion. It thus symbolizes the diverse sources of the rabbinic tradition.

We still have to explain the emergence of the Elders of Bathyra, who are in no way a permanent body. There again Josephus gives himself away: he says that many had come to settle in the colony founded by Zamaris, *for they felt secure there.* Herod persecuted the Pharisees in Judea but did not touch the status of this colony for very clear reasons of general policy regarding the Babylonian Jews and the Parthians, who now ruled Babylonia: the latter were always potentially and sometimes actually enemies of Rome and had invaded Judea in 40 B.C. So it was a refuge, problematic perhaps at times of high drama but in any case precious for all those who could not hope for protection from priestly circles under Herod's sway. In circumstances that are far from clear, an informal and not necessarily permanent coalition was made with the Babylonian Hillel, which certain circles *afterward* regarded as being in succession to the Sanhedrin. No doubt at first a simple fraternity, that is, without professional teachers, this group was later understood as a school and finally as the principal academy.

2. AN ESSENTIAL QUESTION ABOUT PASSOVER

The question put to Hillel provides further information. As we have seen, it is hard to imagine that everyone should have forgotten a precept that applies on average every seven years in the lunar calendar. On the other hand, the question makes no sense in terms of the solar calendar represented in the *Book of Jubilees,* which is independent of the moon and divides the year into four trimesters of sixteen weeks, or 364 days; each trimester begins on a Wednesday (the fourth day of the week), and so 14 Nisan, as we have seen (chap. 2, §II.1), must always fall on a Tuesday and can never coincide with a Sabbath.

There is, however, one situation in which the question has a simple and concrete meaning. If the calendar has just been changed to adopt the lunar system, the concurrence of Passover and Sabbath is going to be a new problem that one day will inevitably arise. If various groups under pressure of persecution had come together at Bathyra—which is perfectly plausible under Herod—it is understandable that in an atmosphere of crisis they should have tried to federate, at least for the time being; but apparently there was no master of recognized authority. In this regard, the choice of Hillel, a Babylonian who had also been a disciple of Jerusalem Pharisees, is in perfect agreement with the spirit of the rabbinic tradition: of the two founders of the school of Yavneh, Yoḥanan b. Zakkai was a Galilean disciple of Hillel, and Gamaliel II was an important Pharisee of Jerusalem.

Hillel's final response is not directly formulated. Perhaps he is chosen precisely because he is prepared to accept differences, or perhaps those who have escaped from Judea will only accept a Babylonian if others adopt the lunar calendar. Whatever the value of these conjectures, the fact remains that it is with Hillel that the rabbinic tradition begins to note *internal* debates, implying subtle differences between diverse traditions: Shammai is inseparable from Hillel, and their "schools" outlasted them. Finally we see how the argument from Scripture is discredited and what importance is accorded to oral tradition. This is particularly visible in a situation of quasi-discontinuity and crisis.

All the same, Hillel's apparent ignorance about Passover is curious and demands an explanation. It is noteworthy that in the discussion he brings forward no Babylonian custom (indeed, none was asked for). There are two ways of interpreting this absence of reference to Babylonia. Passover, as we have seen (chap. 2, §II.3), has two meanings: the commemoration of the deliverance from Egypt and the feast of arrival in the Land. If priority is given to the second aspect, it might seem logical not to celebrate the Passover outside the Land. That would be one way of interpreting Exodus 12:25, which specifies that the rite of the lamb is to be observed "when you have entered into the land that YHWH will give you as he has said." Furthermore, Deuteronomy 16:1ff. demands that the lamb be eaten at the "place that YHWH will choose." If that is taken to mean Jerusalem, it excludes a celebration elsewhere; alternatively, this unique place has not yet been named, which could well suit a sectarian outlook.

Following a second line of interpretation, there are traces of a Babylonian tradition that is strangely ignorant of Passover:

1. The Book of Esther is the foundation narrative of a feast (Purim) commemorating the liberation of Jews, after persecution, *on the spot,* in "Babylonia," whereas in Exodus the liberation of the Israelites is linked to a migration from Egypt toward a Promised Land. At the moment of the oppression, Esther has a three-day fast proclaimed on 13 Nisan (Esth 3:12ff.), which is totally incompatible with the precept of eating the Passover on the 14 Nisan. Of course, it is possible to maintain that the coincidence is only by chance or even, taking into account the lack of certainty about the calendar, that there is no problem. However, we may suspect a controversy, and it is obvious that the standpoint of the narrative is completely different from that implied in the celebration of Passover.

2. The tractate of the Mishnah on the proclamation of the Scripture (*Megila,* "the Scroll") deals first with the scroll of Esther and details the way in which it is to be written, read, and translated; only afterward does it deal with the Pentateuch, by analogy. This remarkable order is the trace of great importance given, at a certain moment, to the feast of Purim. The rabbinic tradition shows that at some point this feast was demoted, so that it gave way to the Sabbath. Symmetrically, the question put to Hillel supposes a context in which Passover has been promoted to be more important than the Sabbath. In the background of a technical debate on the promotion of Passover against Purim, there is obviously an essential problem about the importance to be attached to immigration to the land of Israel or even to pilgrimages. It is not at all unlikely that the Babylonians preferred Purim at home and had little to say on Passover.

The break in continuity that is resolved by Hillel's promotion is not the first of its kind nor the last. It is clear that whereas the inflows from Babylonia are permanent and the spread and popularity of the Pharisee movement certain, especially in the Diaspora, as Josephus emphasizes, the establishment of a Pharisaic continuity in Judea is always very fragile and runs up against both civil and priestly power. The precarious situation of the Pharisees in Judea contrasts with a presence in Galilee that is more stable, though more discreet.

Before and after Herod, the Judaism of Galilee, created by numerous immigrations from Babylonia, was full of life and variety and was strongly rooted in the countryside. The movement properly called "Galilean," in the strict sense of zealot, represents only part of that variety, though a significant part. It is the clear trace, continually renewed through pilgrimages, of a political drive linked to the persistent dream of Jerusalem and the Temple and opposed to the authorities in place in Judea. Herod persecuted the Pharisees in Judea but made many efforts to acquire a Jewish legitimacy, especially in Galilee. He clearly perceived the key position of this remote part of his kingdom. It was in his reign that the exceptional enterprise of Bathyra was founded and that Hillel emerged in a situation of crisis.

III. THE GALILEE THAT JESUS KNEW

Before going on with the history of Galilee, we need to pause. We have already seen enough to be able to form an idea of the Galilean environment in which Jesus recruited his first disciples. This environment was rural, intense, and very different on either side of the lake, which provides a setting for a number of details in the Gospels. It may be helpful to give a short list of characteristic features that clarify the original environment of Jesus and the disciples.

1. In the Gospels Jesus comes from Nazareth, but that is precisely the town that he leaves (we shall discuss later the meaning of the term "Nazorean" and its relation to the place called Nazareth: chap. 5, §II.2). His "own town" was rather Capernaum, on the lake, not far from Tiberias (Mark 2:1; 3:20; 9:33), where archaeological excavations have clearly shown that a fishing village existed before Herod. It was familiar to Jesus, and there he recruited disciples who were experienced fishermen and sailors.

2. Broadly speaking, we have identified an opposition between zealot circles to the west of the Lake of Tiberias and others to the east that were more submissive. This lake plays an important part in Jesus' journeyings, not only from the point of view of geography but also for the symbolism of water and fishing. Besides the theme of crossing the lake, the many references to "the other side" now stand out in relief (see John 6:1 etc.). The symmetrical cursing of Bethsaida and Chorazin (Matt 11:21 par.) includes both sides. The first multiplication of the loaves takes place on the western shore with twelve baskets (Matt 14:13-34 par.), the second on the eastern shore with seven (Matt 15:32-39 par.). These communications between the two shores were not originally meant to build a bridge between the Gentile Decapolis and Jewish Galilee but rather between two opposite tendencies within the same culture. The culture itself was very closed, and Jesus had come only "for the lost sheep of the house of Israel."

3. The environment of reference is rural and religiously highly motivated, with different tendencies engaged in debate or even conflict. The last question put to Jesus by the disciples before

his ascension (Acts 1:6) concerns the restoration of the kingship to *"Israel."* The scene takes place in Jerusalem, and this way of speaking takes no account at all of the real Judea or of Herod's successors. It is rather the trace of a typically zealot dream of liberation, also to be found in the third temptation (Matt 4:8ff.), in the disappointment of the two disciples who leave Jerusalem for Emmaus, and in the choice of Barabbas, who was a "brigand," that is, not a common-law robber but a Galilean of the purest sort, according to Josephus's terminology. Jesus resisted political activism and transformed messianism, or, more exactly, he redefined it in properly biblical terms. On the other hand, while moving about and recruiting in Galilee, he stayed well away from Sepphoris or Tiberias, the only two cities of note in Galilee; they were effectively under Roman control, by way of the Herodian dynasty. To judge from Josephus's vain attempt during the revolt to unify Galilee by overcoming the conflicts between these cities and the intransigent Galileans in the neighboring country districts, it is clear that the environment of Jesus and the disciples is close to that of the "Galileans." This label had very marked connotations, both religious and political, even if Jesus kept his independence.

4. The group that followed Jesus was really very diverse. It included Matthew the tax collector and Simon the zealot (two who were thus in principle opposed and corresponded to the two shores of the lake) and also Joanna, wife of the bailiff of Herod Antipas, representing a third opposed focus, connected with the governing classes of the towns, particularly the new—and shameful—capital Tiberias. Disciples of John the Baptist left him to follow Jesus. In Jerusalem, Jesus had the use of a room for the Last Supper that the disciples did not know about, for they were only there on pilgrimage; so Jesus had other contacts outside Galilee. Controversies between Jesus' disciples and "Pharisees" over purification before eating (cf. Mark 7:1ff.; Luke 11:38) show that they share a common or similar religious culture, which is also close to that of the Essenes; on the other hand, he opposed the Pharisees by maintaining the primacy of Scripture over oral tradition. Some scribes accepted Jesus, while others rejected him; all upheld the Scriptures and were opponents of the Pharisees.

All these tendencies make up a spectrum of the Judaism of Galilee, in which hardly any Sadducees or priests are to be found. Jesus crossed all these barriers, while still remaining within Judaism. He even kept company with "sinners," lepers or prostitutes, but his contacts with Gentiles did not go beyond a few symbolic gestures, which were certainly the maximum that his environment could tolerate. Such gestures were always performed in front of Jewish onlookers; that is the significance of the "sign of Jonah," which was meant for Israelites (even the worst of prophets is capable of converting a Gentile capital, whereas Israel remains stubborn). To this list of transgressions can be added the visit to the Samaritans, who followed the written text and awaited a new Moses and whose recognition of Jesus was one of the most solemn. All these crossings of boundaries taken together signify that Jesus was not afraid of incurring impurity. Fundamentally, he was not afraid of *others*.

5. Just as John the Baptist was surrounded by particular disciples, so was Jesus, who recruited and formed a group. Within it he was acknowledged as the Teacher ("Rabbi"), but it was not a school in the proper sense of the word: the apostles were afterward regarded as folk "without education or culture" (Acts 4:13). That does not necessarily mean that they were ignoramuses, only that they did not fit into any recognized system of doctrinal competence. The group lived a common life, somewhat apart, following its own customs, as illustrated perfectly by the Last Supper. So it was really a fraternity, more or less itinerant, with its own organization, which at the same time undertook to make known to all that the kingdom was close at hand. The Galilean environment was favorable to political ambiguities, as appears even from the written charge fixed to Jesus' cross.

6. Jesus went several times to Jerusalem, alone or in a group. Although critical of the Temple, he never ceased to see in it the center of the promises. At the decisive moment he insisted on confronting the authorities, despite the advice of the disciples (see Matt 16:22 par.). It is entirely possible that some of these had never even made the pilgrimage before, since, though grown-ups, they gazed in wonder at the architecture. Returning from Judea

through Samaria, Jesus foretells the passing of both places of worship, at Jerusalem and on Gerizim (John 4:21ff.), and goes on his way to Galilee. The horizon is once more the Judaism of Galilee, but with some glimpses of broader perspectives.

7. The extreme importance of pilgrimages, which are occasions of encounter and conflict, is emphasized in the Gospels, especially by Luke. Numerous controversies are reported between Jesus and other Jews about the Sabbath, purity, the authority of the oral tradition, etc. However, at his trial no faulty observance was brought forward as a matter for accusation, but solely a charge concerning the Temple, and so pilgrimages. That is significant. Like many others before him, Jesus and his companions had views about the Temple and what it should be, and these views, insofar as they attracted support, were perceived as a threat by the authorities, whether high priest or Roman governor. The fact that they could compare Jesus to Judas the Galilean or Theudas (Acts 5:35ff.) shows where the problem lay.

The sources studied have brought out a number of symbolic and religious factors that explain Josephus's fixation on Galilee. Socioeconomic circumstances, famines, and political oppression also played a part. But those studies of Galilee in this period that regard these material factors as decisive have not been able to come up with any coherent synthesis of the specific features of the local culture, even if they bring into play notions such as "people of the land" or the "poor." They end up by making the historical Jesus a somewhat unreal figure who just happens to turn up in Galilee, but without any traditional roots there.

Jesus was neither the first nor the last "Pharisee" or "Galilean" reformer to get into trouble with the Jerusalem authorities. His profile can be associated with two known religious types that are sometimes opposed: the teacher whose word counts ("rabbi"), as distinct from the scribe, and the Spirit-filled *ḥassid,* well attested in rabbinic sources, whose behavior is sometimes paradoxical and who keeps his distance from learned circles. All those whose origin is known come from Galilee. These *ḥassidim* in fact bear the same name as the Hasideans at the time of the Maccabees (see 1 Macc 2:42). The latter have to be regarded as antecedents both of the Pharisees ("separated") and of the Essenes ("faithful"); before designating different groups, the adjectives had a similar meaning. Neither term can be restricted to the definitions of Josephus, which reflect a situation later than the downfall of Jerusalem. In particular, the Essenes, the *ḥassidim* of Galilee, and the Pharisees of the NT have a number of points in common. Notably, all are able to make the Scriptures speak to the present. So, to further our inquiry, we need to continue our study of the broad outlines of the history of Jewish Galilee.

IV. BEFORE AND AFTER THE DOWNFALL OF JERUSALEM

That Galilee continued to be important in strictly Jewish terms long after the time of Jesus is shown by Josephus's activities there in the war of A.D. 66 and by the establishment in Galilee of the schools that were to produce the normative compilations of the rabbinic tradition.

1. JOSEPHUS AND GALILEE

The difficulties of interpreting the war in Galilee in 66 are well known. Josephus played an important part in it, but the two accounts that he gives, some twenty years apart (*J.W.* 2 §§430ff. and *Life* §§20ff.), are so inconsistent that no firm reconstitution of the facts appears possible. According to both versions, Josephus tried to take in hand the civil authority, at the same time staying on the lookout for any threat from the Romans. In his first and more warlike account, he underlines his effort at civic organization, even giving the impression that he was rebuilding the nation from Galilee, which gives an insight into the importance this region had for him.

Josephus's mission to Galilee can be defined more precisely by looking at his opponents, who were of a quite different type. In the activist Galilean camp he had a rival, John from Gischala in Upper Galilee, who tried to get him recalled by the religious authorities of Jerusalem. In the province at large he had another rival, Justus, who was also seeking to overcome the divisions among the people with a more political agenda; the difference between them was that Josephus tried to do it on the basis of the Galileans of the countryside, while Justus made his bid from Tiberias.

This last point shows clearly what the real mission of Josephus in Galilee was and why it was still of importance so much later in Rome. In action he relies on the rural Galileans, which explains his rivalries with John of Gischala. Later, however, he treats them with disdain: he suggests that their Jewishness is very recent, that the movement of Judas the Galilean was madness, etc. So he was disappointed, and we can see why. Convinced of the supremacy of Rome, he thought in terms of restoring in Galilee a nation that was unified and would accept a reasonable subordination; so he set about reconciling the countrysides (the Galileans) with the towns, which were already subject to Rome.

Josephus failed, principally because of the intransigence of the Galileans, impermeable to political compromise. That was the origin of his vendetta against John of Gischala, the incorruptible representative of this movement, first in Galilee and later in Jerusalem. These Galileans clearly had a very strong identity, social, cultural and religious, just as in the time of the young Herod, who absolutely needed their recognition to establish his legitimacy. John of Gischala also had close relations with notable Pharisees of Jerusalem, in particular Simon b. Gamaliel, father of Gamaliel II, the second founder of Yavneh. Although not zealots, they were akin in views and perhaps in origin, to traditional Jewish Galilee.

2. THE ACADEMY OF YAVNEH

In his *Life,* Josephus really gives no details that explain why he became more pro-Pharisee while remaining distinct from the tendency represented by John of Gischala and Simon b. Gamaliel. Even though he does not mention it, this period corresponds to the birth and development of the academy of Yavneh, which lies at the foundation of the rabbinic tradition.

Two outstanding personalities are at the origin of this institution: the founder, Yoḥanan b. Zakkai, and his immediate successor, Gamaliel II. The town of Yavneh-Jamnia, situated between Jaffa and Ashqelon, and its adjacent territory had been given by Herod to his sister Salome as her personal property. On her death it passed to the Roman empress Livia and then seems to have become the private property of her son Tiberius. Its exact legal status at this time is not entirely clear, but we can at least say that, juridically, it did not form part of Judea. Philo informs us, however, that the majority of the population was Jewish (*Legation to the Emperor Gaius* §§200-203).

In A.D. 68, when the war in Galilee was being extended into Judea, Vespasian brought with him "numerous citizens who had surrendered to him in return for certain rights" and installed garrisons at Yavneh and Ashdod (*J.W.* 4 §130). Later, in circumstances about which Josephus has nothing to say, he put down seditions, in particular at Lod and Yavneh, and "settled there as inhabitants a sufficient number of Jews who had rallied to him" (*J.W.* 4 §444). The connection between the events is uneven, but behind them we can discern an intelligent policy at a moment when disorder was threatening the close of Nero's reign: just as Herod had done with the colony at Bathyra, Vespasian installed Jews who were loyal to him in well-chosen places. They were probably living in fixed residence, or at least under surveillance, but the notable fact is that these Jews came from Galilee.

This is the context in which we can interpret the very fragmentary rabbinic data on the foundation made by Yoḥanan b. Zakkai. There are two versions of the story, which historians have difficulty in reconciling. According to one, he gave himself up to Vespasian, foretold that he would become emperor, and obtained permission to settle at Yavneh with some teachers. The other tells how, having tried in vain, in Jerusalem under siege, to persuade his fellow citizens to give up a hopeless war, he fled the city hidden in a coffin in order to give himself up to Vespasian and obtain concessions. Yoḥanan's active life before Yavneh, known only from rabbinic sources, consists in having kept a school for twenty years at Arab, near Sepphoris, so in Galilee (*YShab* 16:8, p. 15d). He is given as the last disciple of Hillel the Elder (*BMeg* 13a).

This conclusion, which assigns to the school at Yavneh a modest beginning *before* the downfall of Jerusalem, throws light on other points. First, Yoḥanan never cites his master Hillel (or any other), but numerous decisions are attributed to him concerning the calendar or rites, sometimes involving discussions with "the people of Bathyra," that is to say, with the circles of Babylonian origin that had promoted Hillel. So he was not principally a transmitter but, in circumstances that required it, an organizer who encountered a certain amount of opposition. No doubt his school was originally a fraternity without statutory authority over others.

Yoḥanan's successor, Gamaliel II (fl. 90) was of a quite different caliber. His grandfather Gamaliel I, St. Paul's teacher according to Acts, and his father Simon, mentioned by Josephus, were leading Pharisees who were known in Jerusalem. The Mishnah (*MAb* 1:16) presents Gamaliel I in the chain of transmitters, immediately after Hillel (and Shammai), but without indicating any family tie or special master-pupil relationship; indeed it attributes to him the directive to "choose a master for oneself." But any discontinuity is only hinted at: both Yoḥanan and Gamaliel are considered to have inherited the authority of Hillel, who combined, as we have seen, a Babylonian origin (or culture) with the teaching of the Pharisees of Judea, and is thus presented as their common ancestor. So several tendencies have been fused together.

All these details are important, for they help us to characterize Gamaliel II. He reinforced the prestige of Yavneh, got good teachers and students to come there, kept in touch with the Roman authorities, and visited Jewish communities, particularly in Galilee and Rome. His authority allowed other schools, such as Lod, to develop and attracted to Yavneh a spectrum of people of various opinions, as several signs suggest, notably the fact that the Benediction against the "sectaries" was adopted only with difficulty (*BBer* 28b). In point of doctrine, Gamaliel II seems to have combined oral tradition and Scripture, whereas Yoḥanan b. Zakkai, heir to the Babylonian Hillel, admitted only the ancestral traditions.

There was an even more important difference in nature between Yoḥanan's foundation and Gamaliel's enterprise. The former founded only a restricted group, originally of the same dimensions as that of Bathyra. Gamaliel, by contrast, sought to take responsibility for the reorganization of the people after the diasaster of 70. This move had several important consequences: the federation of diverse currents; the respect for Galilee; the insistence on schools rather than on fraternities; and finally, the problem of the "sectaries" *(minim),* who were precisely those that refused or were excluded from federation. Among them were Jewish believers in Jesus. Official Jewish opposition to these latter thus takes a new form. Until this point, it was above all conducted by the Jerusalem authorities; now it will proceed from circles much closer to themselves, but intending to speak for the whole of Judaism.

3. MIGRATION INTO GALILEE AFTER 135

Not much is known about the history of the schools that came out of Yavneh at the end of the first and the beginning of the second century. The evidence suggests that there was wide diversity accompanied by lively debates. There were also cases of exclusion due to diversity of opinions.

After the failure of the uprising led by Simon "Bar Kokhba" (132–135), refugees from Judea emigrated to Galilee. Among them were disciples of Aqiba, who had believed in Bar Kokhba and was put to death cruelly by the Romans. As a teacher he specialized in the attachment of oral traditions to Scripture, and thus in the fusion of different tendencies. An assembly of Aqiba's disciples was held at an unknown date at Usha, not far from Haifa.

This assembly of Usha, without a patriarch, invited the Elders of Galilee to come and study with them (see the midrashic commentary *Canticle Rabbah* 2:16, on Cant 2:5). They came from the east, from a distance of ten to forty miles, which corresponds to a region extending from Sepphoris to the eastern shore of the Lake. The transfer from Yavneh symbolizes a shift of the center of authority and associated institutions. In fact, there are several different signs implying hesitation between Galilee and Judea, which mask oppositions between teachers and tendencies. Politically speaking, two main currents can be distinguished. The adherents of the first, from Judas the Galilean to Bar Kokhba, were intransigent nationalists, opposed to the Romans and even more to Roman influence. Those in the second camp, from Hillel to the assembly of Usha, including also Yoḥanan b. Zakkai and the dynasty of Gamaliel, were just as nationalistic, especially in comparison with Josephus; but despite major doctrinal differences, they were non-political, in the sense of not seeking independence at all costs but only a tranquil vassalage. The assembly of Usha therefore represents a crossroads, immediately after the difficult period under Hadrian, with a certain competition for power.

The center of gravity eventually moved to Tiberias. This city had a strange history. Despite his reconstruction and embellishment of Sepphoris, Herod Antipas, so Josephus tells us, founded Tiberias around A.D. 17–20 over a cemetery, in contradiction with Jewish law. He apparently settled there a mixed population, including Jews forbidden to emigrate, gave them tax advantages, and made it his capital (*Ant.* 18 §§37ff.). Later rabbinic tradition mentions a synagogue at Tiberias and visits by Gamaliel II. Around the middle of the second century, Simon b. Yoḥai, attracted by the thermal baths of nearby Ḥama, proceeded to purify Tiberias, against some opposition. The narrative shows, however, that it was not a cemetery that he purified but the scattered remains of former burial places (*YShebi* 9:1, p. 38d). So Josephus exaggerated his information: when Tiberias was founded, there was no cemetery belonging to a large center of population but just some tombs, and any house might be suspected of being built over one. A century later the reawakening of the suspicion and its resolution by Simon b. Yohai presuppose a development of construction on new terrain.

In all likelihood, Antipas created Tiberias as an act of local politics by settling in a place both central for the Galileans and also perhaps symbolic, if the graves were those of heroes of the resistance. Since he already had a newly rebuilt capital, he must have been trying to place in the heart of traditional rural Galilee an outpost of Roman obedience flaunted inappropriately and aggressively, emphasized by the name of the emperor as well as by its placement over the graves. That could explain the insuperable opposition between the town and the neighboring countryside, which defeated Josephus even as he sought the support of the Galileans. In the next century, after many revolutions, less ambitious sages succeeded where he had failed.

V. FROM FRATERNITIES TO SCHOOLS

We have just been seeing that the environment that produced the Mishnah, although strongly rooted in tradition, underwent some notable developments around the turn of the first and second centuries. In this section we shall look at them in greater detail. To this end, we shall develop further the analogies with the Essenes (and with Jesus' disciples), which have so far been only hinted at. Their true significance comes into focus over the whole matter of purity. In particular, we shall look at two institutions that are especially well defined: the fraternities and proselyte baptism.

1. THE IDEAL OF THE FRATERNITY (ḤABURA)

Rabbinic tradition speaks of an organization of fraternities with exceptionally strict religious requirements. This organization is revered as an ideal, which has left many traces in Mishnaic legislation; but it is not recommended, since by its sectarian structure it introduces an element of selection into the heart of the people. In fact, these fraternities were originally of Essene type, but they came to be regarded rather as schools or academies. This development, whose precise stages are not always clear, is itself the sign of a change of outlook from a sectarian model of renewal to the direction of a whole people.

According to a passage of the Mishnah (*MHag* 2:7), the clothes of the "people of the land" contaminate a "Pharisee" with an impurity like that of the Gentiles. These terms define two quite distinct categories of Jews, and it is clear that these "Pharisees" are rather different from those whom Josephus describes and to whom he says he belongs: they are precisely those who separate from "the people of the land." In the rabbinic context, they are really to be identified with a particular type called *haber,* that is, a member of a special kind of fraternity *(habura),* about which the sources provide a few scattered details.

Certain rabbinical texts (e.g., *TDem* 2:2ff.) divide the people into three classes: (1) the "people of the land," who observe the sabbatical year and the food prohibitions but do not regularly give tithes and do not observe Levitical purity; (2) the "one worthy of confidence" *(ne'eman),* who is scrupulous about tithes; (3) the "associate" *(ḥaber),* who goes even further and eats in a state of Levitical purity, even if he is not a priest. In order to enter one of the two higher classes, the candidate had to pronounce a solemn vow before an "association" *(ḥabura),* a tribunal of three qualified persons or a recognized master. This last stipulation recalls the teacher-disciple relationship that is implicit in the name "Essene" and characterized the followers of John the Baptist and Jesus. As the second class had no organization of its own, it seems to have been only a preparatory phase for the state of *ḥaber,* in which the candidate no longer belonged to the "people of the land" but had not yet become integrated into the association or fraternity. The process of admission seems to have consisted of two phases, each lasting a year: first, access to a certain garment and to pure solid foods, then access to another garment and to pure liquids.

These arrangements are on the whole remarkably similar to the system described by Josephus for admission among the Essenes *(J.W.* 2 §§137ff.), which we shall see in greater detail below (chap. 6, §III.1). They are similar also to the stipulations of the Qumran *Community Rule* 1 QS 6:13-23: period of probation, oaths before the community, and access by stages—first solid foods, then liquids—to the community meal, named precisely "purity." The slight differences that occur are no greater than those involved in the controversies that fill rabbinic tradition. The foods of the fraternities are not specified, and baptisms in the proper sense, marking the stages of admission to the fraternity, are not directly mentioned. On the other hand, as we have seen, the rabbinic tradition marks the importance of bread and wine with special blessings; we shall return to the question of baptism. Once again, we have to do with a religious culture that offers strong analogies with that of the original environment of Christianity.

Whereas the association or fraternity is opposed, like the Essenes, to the rest of the people regarded as perverse, the school sees itself, on the contrary, as representing the whole people. The schools later became normative for all, without any note of exclusiveness, and in particular without expulsion: "A Jew, whatever his sin, remains a Jew." That explains also why the Mishnah is so accommodating and preserves all sorts of traditions that are foreign to its native environment, in particular concerning Jerusalem, the Temple, and the priesthood.

This development from shadowy existence on the fringes to responsibility for a whole people can be seen later in the rabbinical axiom: "Only what the majority of the people can follow should be decreed" (*BBabaB* 60b). It can be seen also in the emergence of a surprising institution known as "proselyte baptism," which we need to examine.

2. PROSELYTE BAPTISM

The question has long been asked if there was a connection between John's baptism and the baptism of proselytes described by rabbinic tradition, because of the obvious similarities. A difficulty arises over dates, since, apart from a few texts that may perhaps allude to some practice of this rite before 70, it is attested neither by the Bible nor by the classical authors Philo and Josephus. With regard to the forced Judaization of the Idumeans and then of the Itureans, Josephus mentions only circumcision. Similarly, he speaks only of the circumcision of Izates, king of Adiabene, then of Azizus, king of Emesa, without any allusion to an immersion (*Ant.* 20 §§34ff. and 139ff.). The most radical solution of this problem is to decide the question with a simple logic: since proselyte baptism cannot have been borrowed from the Christians, it must have existed previously as a Jewish institution. Indeed, the argument continues, it was necessary, as Gentiles were held to be impure and so in need of an immersion. This, however, is to beg the question, for apart from the Essenes, the impurity of Gentiles is mentioned only by the rabbinic sources (see chap. 1, §II.1).

Proselyte baptism is described at length in the Talmud (*BYeb* 47a-b). The ritual presents three remarkable peculiarities. The first is that the baptism takes place after circumcision, and not the other way round; in other words, the neophyte has already become part of the people before he is baptized. That forms an interesting contrast with the discussion in Acts 15:5, where the Pharisees demand unsuccessfully that the newly baptized converts be circumcised so that they may become part of the people. The second peculiarity is that circumcision and baptism form a sort of doublet: each is preceded by a similar preliminary teaching, imparting some grave precepts and some light. There is, therefore, some sort of twofold entry into the Covenant: by circumcision, then by baptism. An interesting comparison can be made with the entry ritual at Qumran (1 QS 6:21 f.), with its associated series of grave and light precepts. The third peculiarity is that there have to be three "witnesses" to the baptism (*BYeb* 46b), contrary to the universal rabbinic principle that two joint witnesses (who are seen by one another) suffice to establish a fact. Among the Essenes, serious matters have to be attested by three witnesses (see CD 9:16-23), but they are not necessarily joint witnesses. More significant is the fact, which we have seen, that the admission of a candidate into the *ḥabura* requires the presence of three qualified members, which suggests rather a tribunal (cf. *MSanh* 1:1). So the "witnesses" of baptism constitute a formal court pronouncing admission.

A	B	C
Essenes and ḥaberim *(candidates already Jews)*	*Rabbinic Judaism (Gentile proselytes)*	*Christianity (Jews and Greeks)*

(The large white circle represents the people, defined by circumcision; the dotted disk, the group that keeps the Covenant, defined by baptism.)

By combining these observations with the conclusions put forward above on the remarkable kinship between the Essenes and the fraternities of *ḥaberim*, it is possible to formulate a very simple hypothesis on the origin of proselyte baptism. The fraternity was originally a reforming sect intent on the renewal of the Covenant for Jews, with initiation and baptisms for the candidates, but not related in any way to entry into the people by circumcision, presumed to have been acquired previously. That is what is represented by figure A in the diagram above. This configuration later develops in two different ways. In rabbinic Judaism (figure B), the fraternity has taken over responsibility for the whole people, after the failure of Bar Kokhba; so, for the proselyte, entry into the people (circumcision) is superimposed on entry into the enlarged fraternity (baptism). By contrast, in Christianity (figure C), access to the fraternity, identified uniquely by baptism, has become independent of whether the candidate has or has not become part of the people by circumcision.

A much-quoted passage (*MPes* 8:8) contains a controversy whose meaning becomes very clear in this perspective: if someone is converted on the eve of Passover, the school of Shammai says that he is then baptized and can take part in the Passover meal the next evening, but the school of Hillel judges that "one who is parted from his foreskin is as if he were coming out of a tomb," so he cannot eat the Passover, since the required ablution takes place later (the third and the seventh days; see Num 19:18ff.). Now, Exodus 12:43ff. stipulates that the uncircumcised cannot share in the Passover. It seems, therefore, that for the school of Shammai, the proselyte is not a Gentile seeking incorporation into the Jewish people but a candidate for admission into the fraternity of the *ḥaberim,* and so has been circumcised long before. On the contrary, for the school of Hillel, the proselyte is a Gentile who must first become part of the people by circumcision (on the eve of Passover in the present case), and hence is impure for seven days. In other words, for the school of Hillel, which has fixed the norm, the reception of the (Gentile) proselyte comprises both circumcision and (later) baptism, the latter act being more or less assimilated to a purification after contact with death and therefore no longer a rite of initiation, properly speaking. This school represents well the extension of the model of the fraternity to the people as a whole. It may not be irrelevant here that in a famous series of stories of Gentiles who ask for instruction, Shammai repels them, whereas Hillel welcomes them (*BShab* 31a).

For figures A and C (Essene and Christian), the true (renewed) Covenant, very important for both groups, implies entry into the small circle; in both cases, too, there is a polemical attitude with regard to the rest of the people. Furthermore, writing about the Essenes, Josephus explains that "if an elder happens to touch a newcomer [a novice], he has to purify himself as after contact with a foreigner" (*J.W.* 2 §150). In other words, since the novice is certainly Jewish, those who do not belong to the community, whether Jews or Gentiles, all have the same degree of impurity. Similarly, a passage in the Mishnah cited above explains that for the *ḥaber* the "people of the land" has the same impurity as a Gentile.

If this opinion is projected onto the first disciples of Jesus, it means that the mission to the Gentiles, like that to the Jews, presupposes the abolition of the *same* ritual barrier. In this precise context, therefore, "neither circumcision nor uncircumcision matters, but new creation" (see Gal 6:15). So, in a climate of crisis, the admission of Gentiles could become thinkable. It may be to exclude such a development that Josephus (*J.W.* 2 §119) insists that the Essenes are "of Jewish birth," an apparently unnecessary stipulation. We therefore arrive at the apparently paradoxical conclusion that the practice of not circumcising Gentile converts to Christianity has its origin not in a "liberal" but in a highly sectarian outlook. Rabbinic Judaism, on the contrary, expressly includes circumcision in the Covenant, which thereby becomes twofold: "As your fathers entered into the Covenant by circumcision, immersion and the casting of blood, so too the proselytes" (*BKer* 9a).

VI. CONCLUSIONS

Jewish Galilee had its own culture, which can already be identified in the days of the young Herod and which persisted long afterward. It was Babylonian in origin by virtue of continual immigrations. Josephus gives more attention to its activist fringe, which was, all the same, rooted in fertile soil.

Everything that we have seen about the religious culture of Jewish Galilee makes it eminently suited to produce rabbinic Judaism. On the other hand, it is less easy to see how it produced the Christianity of the NT. In particular, there is nothing in Jewish Galilee that explains why at a certain point a significant group of Jesus' followers "turned to the Gentiles."

And yet, the religious culture of Jewish Galilee has many institutional features in common both with the Essenes and also with the Christianity of the NT. It seems, therefore, that Christianity originated within a similar environment, from which it retained its most characteristic institutions. The "opening to the Gentiles" constituted a revolution in which, among other effects, the meaning of those institutions radically changed.

We must now investigate this revolution and see if we can account for it.

Chapter Four

The Gentile Mission

Peter's visit to Cornelius (Acts 10) makes no reference at all to any instruction given by Jesus and appears to be unprecedented. That immediately poses the questions of how the Gentile mission was begun and how it was justified. In fact, the primitive community was, as we have seen, so deeply rooted in a Jewish and Galilean environment which was close to that of the Essenes that any opening up to the Gentiles was highly unlikely. It was in very truth a cataclysm, and we need to take the measure of it. Certain passages from the Acts of the Apostles will show the beginnings of this phenomenon in the series of episodes linked with Apollos, Aquila, and Paul at Ephesus and Corinth. But before we look at them, we must see whether there were any currents in the wider Jewish world that might have prepared the way for the Christian Gentile mission. We shall also find that the political and social context in which Christianity began was rather unstable.

I. JEWS AND GENTILES

1. JEWISH PROSELYTISM?

Is there any trace of Jewish proselytism among Gentiles? If so, then it would provide a precedent for the Christian mission. The famous verse of Matthew 23:15, on the scribes and Pharisees who cross land and sea to make one proselyte, has been used to prove the existence of an active Jewish proselytism among the Gentiles. This isolated witness needs, however, to be interpreted.

To obtain greater precision, we first need to draw a distinction between active proselytism (mission) and the acceptance of candidates who come forward on their own initiative. For one thing, no ancient source mentions professional missionaries as a regular Jewish institution, and none laments the fact that Gentiles in general are not Jews. Philo wished to see the spread of the Mosaic Law throughout the entire world; but for that to happen the adherence of Gentile legislators would be enough, without the Jews ceasing to be a distinct people. During the expansion of Judea under the Hasmonean dynasty in the second half of the second century B.C., circumcision was imposed on the peoples and cities incorporated into the kingdom. Marriage with a non-Jew also required the other's conversion for validity. These "normalizations" were, however, simply intended to unify the realm, its laws, and government, under a single jurisdiction. The term "conversion" may not be quite the proper one to apply to these cases, all the more so since their legitimacy was contested in certain quarters.

According to various calculations, it appears that under the emperor Claudius, who ordered a census around A.D. 42, there were in all eight million Jews, of whom two million lived in Herodian Judea (the Roman *Palaestinae* of later times), four million in the rest of the Roman empire, and so two million farther east in enemy territory. (These figures are not certain, but the proportions are probable.) This *ethnos* was fairly mobile, and a constant stream of pilgrims came to Jerusalem, especially for the great festivals. In order to get a true idea of this Jewish population, we need only point out that the total population of the empire at the time would not have been more than seventy million. So the Jews formed an appreciable minority, widely spread, cosmopolitan, and highly visible, to be found especially in the cities of the Diaspora. This healthy demography was due to two factors: natural growth (fortified by the ban on abortion and infanticide) and the arrival of converts.

We are not well informed about how these latter were recruited, but several facts can be mentioned that throw light on possible motives. At Alexandria, it seems, there were preachers in public places. Their audience must have been mixed, as with the numerous synagogues open to all where there was teaching each

Sabbath on virtue and on duty toward God and the neighbor; presumably, the listeners came for religious, ethical, philosophical, or even social reasons. At Antioch, we are told, the Jews, numerous and prosperous since the Hasmonean period, welcomed many proselytes and well-wishers, who were integrated into the people, but there is no suggestion that this was the result of an organized mission among the Gentiles (*J.W.* 7 §45). Likewise, from Josephus we learn that at the same period there had been proselytes at Rome since the time of Augustus (*Ant.* 18 §84). The royal family of Adiabene (*Ant.* 20 §§49-53) was converted by the Bible through contact with Jewish merchants.

Josephus also relates how people from beyond the Euphrates had come at great expense to Jerusalem but did not offer sacrifice when they learned that "Moses forbade it to anyone who does not observe our laws or share our ancestral customs" (*Ant.* 3 §318); they willingly accepted this prohibition, says Josephus, out of respect for Moses. This last case brings out the existence of well-wishers or God-fearers, who were prepared to make costly gestures. They are well attested by Philo and Josephus, by first-century Latin writers, and even by archaeological evidence.

Paul's visit to Athens (Acts 17) is most instructive. He is represented as speaking both in the synagogue and in the public area of the *agora.* His public preaching arouses various reactions; then, when he speaks before the Areopagus to give an official account of the "new religion," he provokes a rejection. The context shows that there was a leisured clientele to listen to preachers of novelties. The failure suggests, however, that direct access to Gentiles, although theoretically possible, was impractical. Elsewhere in Acts, it is clear that the Gentiles among whom Paul's preaching meets with success are God-fearers.

So, too, was Cornelius, whom Peter visited. Justus, to whom Paul goes after leaving Aquila, is another God-fearer, "close to the synagogue" (Acts 18:7). These two scenes are fundamental. Suffice it to note here two remarkable features: they do not take place in the synagogue, still less in public, but in private homes, and they occur on the edge of the spread of a reform movement within Judaism, with more or less well-accepted itinerant preachers. It emerges that internal missionary activity was nothing unusual; according to Acts 13:15, such visitors were regularly permitted to speak in the synagogue.

To sum up, it is clear that there were Gentile converts, but apart from the exceptional case of Judea under the Hasmoneans, their existence is not due to any organized, active proselytism but rather to an attitude of openness in certain Jewish circles, combined with some power of attraction. By contrast, there are clear signs of active proselytism internal to Judaism taking various forms, which we shall now have to examine. Let us note in passing that the invective of Matthew 23:15 against the scribes and Pharisees takes on a simple meaning consistent with Jesus' general outlook; these are reforming groups who are seeking to make new recruits within Judaism. They obviously have much in common with another reformer, namely, John the Baptist. The political fear that he inspired in Herod Antipas (see *Ant.* 18 §118), no less than the charge written by Pilate attributing a political position to Jesus, invites us also to look at the spread of "messianizing" movements in the Jewish communities of the Roman world.

2. REFORMERS AND REBELS

The question of proselytism, therefore, needs to be looked at from the angle of movements internal to Judaism. We shall limit ourselves here to pointing out two large-scale reform movements that were closely related, even though their observable consequences were different: the Pharisees and the zealots, or militant activists.

a) *Pharisee Reformers*

The various accounts that Josephus gives of the Pharisees reflect the changes in his own attitude toward them and so the fluctuations in their fortunes. It is safe to infer that by the time he was writing his *Life,* at least in Rome, the Pharisaic tendency was dominant, or more exactly set the tone. Although this phenomenon had certainly been accentuated by the consequences of the war, it was not entirely new. In 139 B.C. the Jews were expelled from Rome, but they were allowed to return, and Cicero can refer in 59 B.C. to a numerous Jewish minority, emphasizing the strength it gained from its solidarity, but without any suggestion that its presence was illegal. A little later, about 40 B.C., a series of Roman decrees was promulgated in favor of the Jewish communities in the cities around the Mediterranean (*Ant.* 14 §§220ff.), including the authorization of Sabbath rest and dispensation from military service. The communities privileged by the Romans were already well established, but the new measures indicated are in conformity with the pillars of Mesopotamian Judaism and with its oral tradition. This tendency can be broadly called Pharisaic, at least in the primitive sense represented by Nehemiah, at the return from exile, and the Hasideans, at the time of the Maccabean crisis.

These decrees can be put into a precise political context. The Romans were in standing conflict with the Parthians, the ruling power in Mesopotamia (Babylonia), who were seeking to control the whole of Syria and had even succeeded at one time in imposing a king, Aristobulus, in Jerusalem. This was also the moment when Herod got himself appointed king by the Senate, with the mission to reconquer his capital. There were as many Jews living east of the Roman empire as in Judea itself, and it was from those parts that Nehemiah's successors came. So we should conclude that the Pharisaic reform, which obviously presupposes missionaries, had been a success. The strong Oriental influence which that implies could not but worry the Romans, and that is enough to explain their decrees which confer a favor and at the same time remove the beneficiaries from any future conflicts.

That does not, however, mean that even at the time of Josephus observant Pharisees were really in the majority. They had certainly become the reference point, the standard of orthodoxy, as it were. But it would not be the first time that a minority group had served as a standard of reference for a whole people *(ethnos)*, which was juridically well defined but whose piety was in the nature of things variable and occasional. That was the case already with Nehemiah and with the Hasideans.

b) *Militant Activists*

The second wave of "reformers" to have left traces behind can be grouped under the term "zealots," understanding by that what Josephus defines as the "fourth philosophy," connected with Judas the Galilean (*Ant.* 18 §23). The definition that he gives is brief: they have the same doctrines as the Pharisees but accept no human being as master. This Judas was, as we have seen (chap. 3, §I.2), the successor of Ezekias, who had been active in Galilee and whom the young Herod put down, only to be later accused by the Pharisees. We have also seen that these bands of what Josephus calls "brigands" were none other than zealots close to the Pharisees.

Whatever their precise ideals, two characteristic features of these bands constantly stand out, from the beginning of the Roman occupation. For one thing, they aroused division among the Jews, some accepting the movement, others fearing it and denouncing it to the Romans. At the same time, many who joined them were presumably attracted by the prospect of finding an identity while at the same time escaping without danger from paying taxes and from various humiliations, especially in the countrysides and in the poorer quarters of the towns. In other words, such groups would be as unstable as their members' motivation was weak. Hence the occasional rivalries and attempts to outbid one another, such as we see in Jerusalem just before the war: each group defined by a chief and sometimes by a name (*sicarii,* or "assassins," "zealots," etc.).

An excellent example of the ensuing troubles is provided by Josephus himself, in a complex narrative in which he was involved (*J.W.* 7 §§407ff.). After the fall of Masada, *sicarii* who escaped to Egypt provoked sedition at Alexandria, even pursuing the Jews who resisted them. This naturally aroused a very anxious opposition among the leading members of the Jewish community, who finally handed them over to the Romans in order to restore their own reputation with the authorities. Josephus goes on to tell the story of Jonathan, who did the same thing in Cyrenaica. Despite the troubles that Jonathan caused, he managed to denounce the community leaders to the Roman governor, who even got false witnesses to testify against them; in this way many rich people were executed and their goods confiscated. The historian explains that he himself was among the accused, but the matter reached Rome, where Vespasian whitewashed him. He is certainly tendentious, but he brings out well both a mechanism of serious divisions among Jews, with physical coercion and Roman punishments, and also the eagerness of the Romans to exploit these divisions in order to strengthen their own power, which does not seem to have been all that secure.

These phenomena were not new in Josephus's time. Conflicts within Judaism were a constant reality. There was always, in one form or another, a party faithful to the Law, and another more political one, negotiating for advantages with the suzerain power, first Seleucid, then Roman. The "observant" party, by nature non-political (e.g., the Hasideans), always has an activist fringe that rejects the "collaborators" (e.g., Mattathias and Judas). The personalization of the groups was a constant feature. When the high priest says, "It is better for one man to die for the people rather than for the entire nation to perish" (John 11:50), he judges that the initiator of a group only needs to disappear for the whole group to dissolve. Gamaliel's argument (Acts 5:36ff.) is of the same nature.

The problem, however, was on a much bigger scale, as is shown by the case of Jonathan in Cyrenaica, as well as the proportions taken by the project to place Caligula's effigy in the Temple, around A.D. 40, which we shall see shortly. If there were so many leaders with varying success, if local problems were all the time getting out of hand, there must have been widespread tensions that drew a notable following toward the agitators.

3. *CHRISTIANI* AT ROME, ALEXANDRIA, ANTIOCH

This is not the place to analyze the social tensions in the Roman world but only to take notice of certain Jewish phenomena that keep recurring in the great cities. We shall look first at the main ones—Rome, Alexandria, and Antioch—which we shall take in that order for purely practical reasons.

Rome. In A.D. 19, Emperor Tiberius banished all the Jews from Rome, states Josephus, because of the crimes committed by four of them (*Ant.* 18 §84). A major crisis seems to have been sparked off by an episode that was quite minor in itself. Josephus's information seems partial, in both senses of the word.

Nonetheless, the whole affair has a strong odor of what he would call "brigandage," namely, zealot agitation in the name of the Law, whose very visible socio-political fallout obliged the Romans to react. Later on, Claudius, according to Suetonius (*Claudius, §*25), expelled from Rome Jews who were stirring up constant tumults at the instigation of "Chrestus" *(impulsore Chresto)*. Suetonius gives no date, but by combining what he has to say with other texts, we can conclude that the events reported are to be placed in the first year of the emperor's reign, that is, 41. Before even envisaging who this "Chrestus" might be, let us first look at a highly important scene that converges with the text of Suetonius, namely, the meeting between Aquila and Paul at Corinth (Acts 18:1ff.), in which the WT (right-hand column) and the AT (left-hand column) show characteristic differences.

(**18:**1) *After leaving Athens, Paul arrived at Corinth.*

(2) Having found a certain Jew named	*(2) Having found*
Aquila, originally from Pontus, who had recently arrived from Italy,	*Aquila, originally from Pontus, a Jew who had recently arrived from Italy*
and Priscilla his wife,	*with Priscilla his wife, he greeted them with joy. They had left Rome,*
for Claudius had ordered all the Jews to depart from Rome,	*for Claudius Caesar had ordered all the Jews to depart from Rome; they had emigrated to Achaia.*
(3) he attached himself to them. And, through their being of the same trade,	*(3) Paul was known to Aquila through their being of the same kind,*
he stayed with them, and they were working. They were tent makers.	*and he stayed with him.*

Between the WT and the AT, Aquila undergoes some interesting transformations. For the AT, he is fairly harmless. An unremarkable sort of person, he has come from Italy, without further specification, rather than precisely from Rome. He works quietly at a trade that he and Paul have in common and gives Paul a base and somewhere to live. That is all. We can even guess already that he will become a disciple of Paul, as the narrative goes on to imply. Things are quite different in the WT. There Paul and Aquila are of the same "kind"; the Greek word means literally "tribe," but the context suggests something more than simply being Benjaminites, and in fact the term can refer to any group with a common bond. Of the two, the more important is Aquila, since the fact that Paul is known to him is significant. Aquila and Paul need not have been personally acquainted. Information must have circulated within the movement, especially among the ports around the Mediterranean basin, which were always in touch with Rome. The expression "having found" then takes on its true meaning: Paul, with a rumor going before him, was looking for Aquila in order to find support for his own action. But that is not all. Aquila does indeed come from Rome. Claudius's edict of expulsion enables us to be precise enough: the government was expelling troublemakers, who were creating "disturbances," and Aquila was one of them, and not the least. In other words, this is the Paul who was noted for his aggressive zeal for the Law (see Phil 3:6; Acts 22:3). The account in Acts does not mention the name of Jesus. If Paul spoke to Aquila about Jesus, it would have been as the Messiah of a zealot movement.

That Aquila and Paul belonged to the same movement has a very important consequence. In fact, if Suetonius's formula *impulsore Chresto* characterizes the disturbances repressed by Claudius in 41, those troubles certainly date back much earlier, since they are described in terms of a constant agitation; we would not go far wrong in attributing them to the provocative policies of his predecessor, Caligula. In that case the Chrestus mentioned by Suetonius, though definitely Jewish, is unlikely to have been Jesus. So, then, who was this person, real or imagined, who aroused revolts?

The first point to make is that it is not directly a question of "Christians" but only of Chrestus (or Christus: at this time these two Greek words were pronounced identically). Later on, in 64, in the context of the fire at Rome under Nero, the same Suetonius speaks clearly of the *christiani* and their new and harmful *superstitio* (*Nero* §16). Tacitus reports the same events in a famous passage in which he expressly distinguishes the popular name *chrestiani* from the name of the founder, Christus, put to death by Pontius Pilate (*Annals* 15.44). Something has happened between these two dates: the *chrestiani* are now the followers of a definite person called Christus (Tacitus is unaware of any link with the title "Messiah").

The conclusion is clear. First, Suetonius's Chrestus in 41 A.D. does indeed refer to the Jewish Messiah. The identification of this figure with Jesus comes only later, but the Romans react in both cases in an identical way. This allows the interpretation of two literary details. Tacitus links a popular name *(chrestiani)* and a definite person *(Christus),* but the spelling suggests that there were indeed *chrestiani,* that is, "partisans of (the) Christus/Chrestus" or messianists, before the link with Jesus was made. For his part, Suetonius speaks of instigation, or literally, "impulsion," and not of real command or leadership. In other words, the Messiah exercises an influence in his absence, which suggests that the leaders were proclaiming the imminent coming of a messianic kingdom.

This result allows us to recognize a common character in all the similar movements that appear in turn, starting with Ezekias under Herod. Time and time again people who are religiously highly motivated, though militarily very weak, dare to stand up to the power of Rome or its representatives and carry with them a great number of Jews who are attracted also by the idea of avoiding oppressive taxes. Unless we assume that they are simply crazy, the only plausible explanation is that, in all cases, they are proclaiming that the end of time or the kingdom of God or else the messianic era is close, and doing so with conviction, based on a well worked-out interpretation of the Scriptures. The imminent coming of the Messiah gives a major impulsion, and at the same time it seriously divides the Jewish community, since those who do not accept the message see how dangerous it is.

Alexandria. Shortly after he came to the throne in 41, Claudius replied to the official good wishes sent by the citizens of Alexandria (*PLond* 1912; see *Corpus Papyrorum Judaicarum* II, n° 153). Among other things, he expressed his will concerning the Jews. After mentioning recent troubles amounting to war against them (or some of them), he began by confirming their privileges, then announced certain measures he was taking in their regard. In particular, he forbade them to bring in Jews from Syria or Egypt and also to send two lots of official representatives to Rome. So the disturbances had been instigated or fomented by newcomers to the Jewish community of Alexandria; the result was repression and then a visible division of the community, serious enough to worry the government at Rome, where similar troubles had recently broken out. Such a split is quite distinct from the emergence here or there of tiny groups meeting in private, such as we see in Acts. On the contrary, through Claudius's letter we glimpse the sudden appearance of widespread and dangerous popular movements aroused by agitators with a simple religio-political message.

The situation at Alexandria resembles that at Rome in its effects and in its causes, even though the idea of "Messiah" is not expressed in the emperor's letter. In Acts, Alexandria does not feature in the itineraries of Peter or Paul, which may sufficiently explain why that city is hardly mentioned. On the other hand, it was at Alexandria that Apollos got to know "the things concerning Jesus," as well as the baptism of John, but without a messianic dimension, as we shall shortly see. That forms a contrast with the situation glimpsed at Rome, where messianists and the heritage of Jesus were fused some time between 41 and 64.

Antioch. It was here, according to Acts 11:26, that for the first time the disciples were called "Christians." The first thing to note is that the name *Christiani,* with the sense of "partisans of (the) Christus," is of Latin, not Greek, formation, and that the formulation of the sentence in Acts has an official ring about it. The name may well be of popular origin, but it is likely that its use here, with its juridical coloring, comes more immediately from the Roman authority. It is given (imposed) for the first time at Antioch, and it will mark its bearers as criminals; perhaps it already did so before it was applied to the disciples of Jesus.

What has taken place? As we have already seen, the Jewish community of Antioch had for a long time been prosperous, peaceful, and open. It welcomed Gentiles, who could be regarded as integrated into the people, even though neither they nor their children are said to have been circumcised (*J.W.* 7 §45). However, the affair of Caligula's statue had a major impact there. In the winter of 39–40, Petronius, governor of Syria, received an order from the emperor to go to Jerusalem and install his statue in the Temple by force. Philo tells us (*Leg.* §§185ff.) that the Jews of Antioch were the first to get wind of the affair. Then, according to Josephus, Petronius, on his way to Jerusalem, met with Jewish opposition, which was total though non-violent, at Ptolemais and Tiberias (*Ant.* 18 §261ff.). There were, however, disturbances at Antioch at the same time or even before that involved Jews and were put down with severity. Did these concern the same affair, or were they a messianic agitation, as at Rome, or perhaps violent reactions to preaching about Jesus?

Acts 11:19-26, taken in three sections, preserves the trace of several missions to Antioch (the AT, on the left, is given only when it contains a different reading from the WT that is significant for the present discussion).

A   (19) *On the one hand, those who had been scattered by the storm that broke out through Stephen went as far as Phoenicia, Cyprus and Antioch, speaking the word to no one*

but only to the Jews. | *but to Jews alone.*

(20) *On the other hand, there were men from Cyprus and Cyrene, who having gone to Antioch, were speaking*

also to the Hellenists | *to the Hellenes (Greeks),*

proclaiming the Lord Jesus. (21) The hand of the Lord was with them: a great number having become believers turned to the Lord.

B   (22) *The matter concerning them came to the ears of the church of Jerusalem, and they sent Barnabas to Antioch. (23) He, having arrived and seen the grace of God, rejoiced, and he exhorted them all to remain profoundly attached to the Lord. (24) He was indeed an upright man, filled with Holy Spirit and with faith. A considerable crowd joined themselves to the Lord.*

C   (25) | *Having heard that Saul was*
He went to look for Saul at Tar- | *at Tarsus he went to look for*
sus. (26) And having found him | *him. Having joined him he*
he brought him | *asked him to*

to Antioch. It happened	come to Antioch. Having
that during an entire year	arrived, during an entire year
they were gathered	they were gathered
in the church	to the church
and instructed a	and instructed a
considerable crowd,	considerable crowd.
and that for the first time at An-	Then for the first time at
tioch the disciples were called	Antioch the disciples were called
Christiani.	Christiani.

In the AT, the first section (A)—"speaking to the Jews and also to the Hellenists"—is, to say the least, ambiguous. By contrast, the WT indicates two distinct movements ending at Antioch, one starting in Jerusalem and addressed only to Jews, the other starting from Cyprus and Cyrene and addressed to Greeks (Gentiles). What is going on here? We may get an idea by bringing together the following points. (1) The final "proclamation" in verse 20 has the effect of blending the two movements together by attributing the same message to both. (2) On the other hand, in verse 21, the expression "turn to the Lord" is the same as that in James's decree (see Acts 15:19), where, as we shall see (chap. 5, §I,1), it concerns the Gentiles; it is indeed the continuation of verse 20, but there was originally no connection with Jesus. (3) The propaganda addressed to the Greeks becomes more precise when we consider all together the great number of recruits, the fact that at Antioch the Jews had numerous Greek well-wishers, and also the fact that the missionary movement originated in Cyrenaica, which recalls the disturbances in Alexandria. (4) The preachers are anonymous and are not known from elsewhere as disciples. (5) A "considerable crowd" is mentioned twice. (6) Those won over by the preaching are described by the Roman term *Christiani.*

The whole of this passage can be put into the context of the disturbances caused by Caligula's plan to place his statue in the Temple at Jerusalem. In this hypothesis, Jewish preachers came to arouse among the Greeks, perhaps with a note of eschatological urgency ("The Messiah is coming"), a lively reaction against this abuse of the cult of the emperor, a reaction that was probably sharpened by other abuses of Roman power. Antioch was the seat of the Roman government of Syria, and it is not difficult to imagine demonstrations against Petronius in the winter of 40. From a Roman point of view, they would have taken place *impulsore Chresto,* and from a Jewish point of view, it would all have amounted to a visible and promising act of renunciation of idols.

This hypothesis is reinforced by the mission of Barnabas (part B). It is recounted in lyrical fashion, insisting on the qualities of Barnabas. Two important details, however, stand out. It is a "matter" which comes to the knowledge of Jerusalem but which was not initiated there, and now needs to be looked into. Then Barnabas exhorts the "considerable crowd" to remain faithful. In other words, the amazing success might turn out to be no more than a flash in the pan, unlikely to prove durable, especially if there were a severe repression. What is really remarkable is the absence of any reference to Jesus or baptism or any union between Jews and Gentiles. On the contrary, the mission to the Jews at Antioch in verse 19 appears to be entirely independent of the other, and no coordination is established between them. Coming also from Jerusalem, it makes up a diptych: the missions to the Jews and to the Gentiles are distinct and apparently without conflict, which fits in perfectly with the position of James (see Gal 2:9).

Saul's intervention (part C) is essentially one of backing up and giving substance to the action taken by Barnabas, which seems to have developed beyond his original mission. For the WT, Barnabas, "filled with Holy Spirit and with faith" but not seeing how people from Jerusalem can be of much help in the situation, thinks of Saul, with his reputation as an activist, as the most appropriate person to call in. It is presumably Saul, the future apostle Paul, who proclaims to Gentiles at Antioch that the Messiah, to whose cause they have in some sense been won, is Jesus. In the revised version represented by the AT, it appears to be well known that Saul is at Tarsus, and Barnabas seems to be more securely in charge of his mission and keeps the initiative.

The involvement of the disciples in the disturbances that took place at Antioch in 39–40 was apparently noticed by the Romans and gave the movement that Barnabas was trying to manage the name of "Christian." The Jews reached by the mission mentioned in verse 19 probably found themselves also included in this category. (Decoded: Jewish disciples who were not zealot activists have been assimilated to the messianists, that is to say, accused of subversive activities.)

This long detour through three great cities of the Roman world has brought out the picture of a Jewish messianism whose outline can be discerned by following the Roman reactions to the disturbances that it caused, especially under Caligula. At its center was an eschatological urgency, but this was filled out by associated particular interests (such as avoidance of taxes); it gave rise to insurrection in the Jewish community and also among Gentile proselytes and well-wishers, especially at Antioch. Originally, this messianism had no identifiable connection with Jesus and his successors; later, once the link was established in the confused situation at Antioch, the criminal label of "Christian" was attached indelibly to Jesus' disciples, which presupposes some intrinsic and durable link. Two questions then arise about this messianism, and we are going to study them further by following the Jerusalem-Asia Minor axis, which is better documented than the three great cities: Why did a rumor of Jesus as Messiah spread in this way? And why did Jesus' disciples make use of it, despite the scandal of a crucified Messiah?

Adjacent to these questions is the observation that the social body of the disciples develops on two tracks: alongside little groups of believers are crowds large enough to worry the Roman authorities. The connection between the two entities is still not very clear. That was already the reality surrounding Jesus in the Jewish world.

II. EPHESUS AND CORINTH

The narratives of Acts 18–19 appear to provide a detailed account of the evangelization of Corinth and Ephesus, in which Paul has the principal role. In reality, these chapters are a more or less coherent collection of small narrative units with different origins. Let us now try to unscramble some of them by following first Aquila and Apollos, the main persons who are mentioned alongside Paul, apparently as his fellow workers.

1. APOLLOS AND CORRECT TEACHING

We have already seen Aquila's first appearance on stage. He is a messianizing Jew whom Paul finds at Corinth and who had been expelled from Rome under Claudius in 41. In order to get a better idea of him, we shall first study a scene from which Paul is absent: a certain Apollos from Alexandria teaches at Ephesus in the presence of Aquila and his wife Priscilla, who then put him right. The text is not without its problems and has undergone a number of changes in the course of reinterpretation. As before, we place the WT on the right when it differs significantly from the AT:

> (**18**:24) *A Jew called Apollos, from Alexandria (AT adds by nation), an eloquent man, had arrived at Ephesus, being powerful in the Scriptures.* (25) *He had been catechized*

| | *in his own country* |
| *in the* way *of the Lord* | *in the* word *of the Lord* |

> *and filled* (lit. "boiling") *with the Spirit he was holding forth and teaching exactly the things concerning Jesus, knowing only the baptism of John.* (26) *He began to teach with assurance in the synagogue. Having listened to him,*

| *Priscilla and Aquila took him aside, and expounded to him more exactly the way of God.* | *and expounded to him more exactly the way.* |

This brief narrative gives rise to a number of problems. According to the AT, Aquila and Priscilla simply give greater precision to Apollos's teaching, which amounts only to a difference of degree in his knowledge of the "way of God," an expression in itself fairly banal. It is not said whether these additional items concern Jesus. For the WT, Apollos did not know "the way" but only "the things concerning Jesus." In what follows, he is instructed in "the way" (without "of the Lord" or other complement). This expression occurs elsewhere in Acts (Acts 9:2; 19:9, 23; 22:4; 24:14, 22), most often to designate the disciples of Jesus and always in a context of disturbance in which Paul is involved. The notion of "way" refers essentially to preparing for the final coming of God, according to Isaiah 40:3. It already featured, along with the return to the desert, in the preaching of John the Baptist (Matt 3:3 par.) and is found in the same form in the Qumran *Community Rule* (1 QS 8:12ff.).

This goal of preparing the way can, however, split into two very different attitudes: either fervent observance of the Law (call to conversion, etc.), with a course of initiation, as with the Essenes, or messianizing activism, wanting to get rid of evil by force, as with the "brigands." Apollos obviously belongs to the first type, acquainted as he is with John's baptism and with Jesus; Aquila belongs no less obviously to the second, as one who has been expelled from Rome, but he is the one who speaks of the "way." Apollos is not a personal disciple of John but has encountered John's baptism at Alexandria. He belongs to a group for whom Jesus is a teacher and healer. What Aquila proposes to Apollos is certainly a reinterpretation of the nature of what he already knows about Jesus (who is not called Christ or Lord), and this development brings Apollos closer to Aquila. Already at Corinth (Acts 18:1ff.), it seems, Aquila, like Paul at Damascus (Acts 9:20) and under his influence, has come to acknowledge Jesus as the Messiah who is shortly to return. Accordingly, he instructs Apollos with a more messianizing view of Jesus.

The "exactness" that is required and verified is a technical term normally used for checking the accuracy of a (handwritten) book. In this case, Aquila is checking the accuracy of an oral teaching, according to a technique attested in the rabbinic tradition. Apollos has already been "catechized," so he has received an oral teaching, and Aquila's intervention is also oral.

The entire episode is to be dated after Aquila's arrival in Corinth, which was connected with Claudius's decree of 41. That is also the period of his letter to the Alexandrians which, as we have seen, tries to restore order to messianic agitations. Apollos comes from Alexandria to Ephesus as an itinerant preacher, but there is no reason to think he had been expelled or that he was suspect in the eyes of the authorities. However, after his meeting with Aquila, he begins to proclaim that the Messiah is Jesus, and a few difficulties occur. Once again the narrative has been much reworked in the AT:

(**18**:27)	At Ephesus were residing some Corinthians. Having heard [Apollos],
[Apollos] wishing to make the voyage to Achaia, the brethren, having approved, wrote to the disciples to welcome him.	they asked him to make the voyage with them to their country. He gave his consent, and the Ephesians wrote to the dis- ciples of Corinth that they might welcome him.
He, once arrived, was a great resource to those believing by grace,	He, having left for Achaia, was a great resource in the assemblies,

(28) *for he was refuting vigorously the Jews, in public, (WT adds debating), showing by the Scriptures that the Messiah is Jesus.*

The account in the AT is both flat and uselessly complicated. There were disciples at Corinth, as the reader of Acts has known since 18:8. Then Apollos has the happy idea of going to Achaia (whose capital was Corinth), where he is able to be of help in difficult public discussions. At the most one might wonder what the exact point of the letter sent from Ephesus was. The grace that surrounds Apollos makes one think of Stephen, who was also "filled with grace and power" and stood up to the Jews in debate (Acts 6:8-10). Nothing really new, then.

The WT is profoundly different. First, there were indeed disciples at Corinth, certainly Jews, and some of them were impressed by Apollos when they heard him at Ephesus. Apparently the novelty of his message consisted in showing that the Messiah is Jesus, with eloquence and texts to make the point. But what sort of disciples were they? The business about the letter is indeed strange: the Corinthians who bring Apollos with them need a guarantee from the Ephesians! Ephesus was, of course, a great center, with an ancient Jewish community enjoying long-established privileges, whereas that at Corinth was more recent and may have been founded from Ephesus. But the real problem lies elsewhere: these Corinthians from Ephesus have grounds to fear that they will be disowned by the disciples at Corinth, that is, by their own brethren.

In other words, Apollos is now a problem person, capable of provoking divisions at Corinth. The conclusion of the narrative then falls into place very easily: whether or not he really got as far as Corinth, he has shown himself to be a good advocate in the "assemblies."

Once again, there is an obvious comparison with Stephen, but we can see more clearly why he provoked such violent reactions. Opposition could come on two fronts: from Jews, whether or not they were disciples of Jesus, who did not accept messianism or were afraid of it, or from messianists who did not accept the reference to Jesus. It is interesting to observe that the Corinthians who invited Apollos are not described as disciples and that they disappear in the AT; likewise, the Ephesians who write the letter are not recognized as community leaders and become "brethren" in the AT. There is a hint of different parties among disciples of Jesus who owe nothing to Paul, and so it is understandable that the AT has shortened and watered down a narrative that gave evidence of divisions. Finally, we note that in all the discussions there is no mention of the missions to the Gentiles; there is no reason to think that they were among the additional points made by Aquila to Apollos.

There are later traces of divisions centering on Apollos. Paul denounced disagreements among Corinthians in 1 Corinthians 1:12, where some are for Paul, others for Apollos, still others for Cephas, and others again for "the Christ." Later on he says that he planted, Apollos watered, and God gave the increase, but adds that he himself is the real father (1 Cor 4:15). Finally, he states that he and Apollos serve as an example for the brethren not to take sides against one another and to learn the principle "Nothing beyond what is written." Paul does not say or imply that he and Apollos say the same thing. Quite the contrary in fact. But rather than underline the differences, which were surely real enough (see 1 Cor 16:12), he takes another point of view, which puts all preachers on the same level and makes all their quarrels futile, namely, the reality of the cross of Christ. This "spiritual" method of overcoming contradictions and conflicts, which Paul uses here (and elsewhere), shows that he is no longer the same man who sought out Aquila, precisely at Corinth, a city with a tradition of

agitation and division that lasted until the time of Clement of
Rome! For the moment let us simply notice the fundamental
change in Paul expressed by one text: he now speaks of Jesus
Christ risen as Lord (1 Cor 1:2ff.).

What has happened? Just as Apollos's development could be
traced by an itinerary from Ephesus to Corinth, that of Paul can
be followed by going in the opposite direction.

2. PAUL, FROM CORINTH TO EPHESUS

We shall limit ourselves here to following Paul's relations
with Aquila and his interventions in Ephesus. In fact, Paul parted
from Aquila at Corinth, on the occasion of a crisis provoked by
his preaching (WT on the right):

(**18**:4a) *He was holding forth in the synagogue each Sabbath.*	*Entering the synagogue each Sabbath he was holding forth, introducing the name of the Lord Jesus.*
(4b) *He was persuading Jews and Greeks. . . .*	*He was persuading not only Jews but also Greeks.*
(5b) *Paul devoted himself to the word, attesting to the Jews that the Messiah is Jesus.*	
(6) *These opposing and blaspheming,*	(5b) *Many words being spoken and the Scriptures being interpreted, certain Jews were opposing and blaspheming.*
after tearing his garment, he said to them: "Your blood is on your own head; as for me, I am pure. From now on I will go to the nations."	*Then Paul, after tearing his garment, said to them: "Your blood is on your own head; as for me, I am pure. Now I am going to the nations."*
(7) *Then withdrawing from there, he went to one called Titius Justus, a God-fearer, whose house adjoined the synagogue.*	*Then withdrawing from Aquila's, he took refuge with Justus, a God-fearer. His house adjoined the synagogue.*

The AT gives a very simple account. After some interest in his message has been shown by both Jews and Gentiles, Paul devotes his efforts to the Jews. When they reject him totally, he pronounces something like a curse inspired by Ezekiel 33:2-9 and ends by announcing a future mission to the Gentiles, then takes himself off to a Gentile God-fearer. Such a declaration by Paul is not new in Acts: in 13:46, with Barnabas at Antioch of Pisidia, he announced that he was going to the Gentiles, but that did not prevent him from systematically visiting the synagogues wherever he went. What is new here is that he goes to stay with a God-fearer, a point that recalls the episode of Peter and Cornelius. The theme that provoked the rejection was the testimony that "the Christ is Jesus." In the context of the AT it is difficult to see in it a properly messianic proclamation; it is rather a Pauline kerygma witnessing to the resurrection.

The WT presents a quite different image. The first and essential point is that Paul provokes a division among the Jews. Only two items of his message are given: there was discussion, copious and perhaps confused, about the Bible, and he "introduced the name of the Lord Jesus." This second feature, which does not contain the term "Christ," is suspect. For the WT, Paul, like Aquila, is a messianist. This accounts for the mixture of excitement, biblical debates, and divisions; later a glossator with good intentions added a phrase showing that to talk of the "Messiah" Paul added "Jesus" and "Lord," that is, Jesus as Lord and not only as Messiah.

Finally, the fact that in the WT Paul declares "Now I am going" and leaves Aquila for the house of a God-fearer looks very much like a movement of anger, accompanied by a significant transgression (entering a Gentile's house). In what follows, verses 18-21 explain that Paul arrives in Ephesus with Aquila (and Priscilla) and leaves them there, but commentators have for a long time regarded these as secondary touches that prepare for the meeting between Aquila and Apollos in this city. Aquila is under Paul's orders, and so Apollos will receive sound teaching. In reality, Paul has split up with Aquila, who never says that he will go to the Gentiles and who certainly did not recommend Apollos to do so.

Following back from the AT to the WT, we can make out a picture of Paul as a messianizing activist. This scene is told after the episode at Antioch, which we have already examined, which itself follows the incident on the road to Damascus. That episode took place before 39, while the meeting with Aquila occurred in 41. Our conclusion would be that Paul already believed that the Messiah whose return was imminent was Jesus but that this belief had not yet brought about any further change in his fundamental position.

3. THE DISCIPLES AT EPHESUS

In fact, we find Paul again shortly afterward at Ephesus (we leave aside insignificant differences between WT and AT):

(**19**:1)	Paul wishing of his own will to go to Jerusalem, the Spirit told him to return to Asia.
It happened, while Apollos was at Corinth, that Paul, having gone through the high-lands, went to Ephesus and there found some disciples. (2) *He said to them:*	*Having gone through the high-lands, he comes to Ephesus* (2) *and says to the disciples:*

"Did you receive the holy Spirit when you became believers?" But they: "But we have not heard that there is a holy Spirit." (3) He said to them: "In view of what have you been baptized?" The others said: "In view of John's baptism." (4) Paul said: "John baptized with a baptism of conversion, saying to the people 'in view of the one coming after him,' so that they might believe—that is in Jesus." (5) Having heard that, they were

baptized in the name of the Lord Jesus.	*baptized in the name of the Lord Jesus for the remission of sins.*
(6) *And Paul having laid (his) hands on them, the holy Spirit came on them.*	(6) *And Paul having laid (his) hand on them, the Spirit fell on them.*

| And they were speaking in tongues, and they were prophesying. | They were speaking in tongues, and themselves interpreting them and they were prophesying. |

(7) *All these men were about twelve.*

This passage has the reputation of being difficult, especially regarding the identity of the disciples. But let us continue with the method employed up till now of looking closely at the differences between AT and WT.

In the perspective of the AT, Apollos arrives in Corinth after Paul has left, which agrees with 1 Corinthians 3:6. At Ephesus, Paul finds some disciples who are totally unaware of the Holy Spirit, and he brings them up to date. The episode appears to be an atypical leftover from an earlier tradition, dealing perhaps with some "disciples of John the Baptist." They can hardly be disciples of Jesus, since Paul, Aquila, and Priscilla have just been through Ephesus and laid the foundations of a Christian community. The group is small, which brings out Luke's concern not only for large numbers but even for a dozen or so individuals. By baptism in the name of Jesus and the gift of the Spirit, they are brought into contact with Pentecost (see Acts 2:41), thanks to Paul. Thus everything is in order, and the development of the Church is all of a piece.

Comparison with the WT brings out the fact that the passage has been reworked, and the interpretation just given breaks down. First, Paul has been turned aside from his plan to go to Jerusalem, with a remarkable contrast between what he himself wanted and the impulse of the Spirit making him turn back in his tracks. Then, at Ephesus he speaks to the disciples, who number exactly twelve according to some manuscripts, and tells them about the Spirit. There is no connection with the following episode, in which Paul goes to the synagogue at Ephesus for three months. In this brief narrative we get a new image of Paul. For the first time he speaks of the Spirit; for the first time he addresses disciples without messianist language or disorderly scenes. These new features can only be connected with the Spirit who makes him turn back and indeed turns him round. It is even possible to speak of a (second) conversion: Paul's way of viewing Jesus has undergone a profound transformation.

We have described these twelve as disciples of Jesus. However, they had been baptized "in view of John's baptism." Thus these disciples are in the same position as Apollos: within groups defined by John's baptism, Jesus is a teacher and healer but not the definitive liberator. In other words, there is no major difference at this stage between being a disciple of John or a disciple of Jesus (see John 3:23). Jesus' disciples are simply a subgroup of the same type, whatever the personal qualities of Jesus himself. Paul now tells them that John was proclaiming Jesus. To be more precise, John was proclaiming a baptism in view of the one who would come after him so that they might believe. This successor would be the definitive liberator, whatever the precise label attached to him, and to "believe" means to enter into baptism (or be admitted to it). Paul tells them that the definitive liberator is Jesus.

If that were all, Paul would have given the disciples at Ephesus the same messianizing view of Jesus that Aquila gave Apollos. But in the present narrative two things happen to the disciples that did not happen to Apollos: they are baptized "in the name of Jesus" and they receive the Holy Spirit. So Paul's message is no longer the same as Aquila's. We can now understand the meaning of his question, whether they had received the Holy Spirit when they became believers: it is only in the Spirit that the true identity of Jesus can be perceived. When they reply that they have not heard that there is a Spirit, they are not talking about the divine Spirit in general. Rather, they have not received the power to recognize that Jesus is this definitive figure whom John proclaimed and that they are even now in his kingdom, for he is living. This is one of many ways of talking about the resurrection, different from the empty tomb ("the earth has yielded its fruit") but resembling the final scene in Matthew: "I am with you until the end of time" (28:20).

Paul himself does not confer the "second" baptism. He lays on his hand(s), and the effect of the Spirit is an unaccustomed language, at once glossolalia (lack of meaning) and prophecy (excess of meaning), which shows that the Spirit is none other than that of the Prophets. His gesture puts a closure on a course leading to admission, which is precisely "baptism," reformulated in the name of Jesus but still, like John's, conferred "for the remission of sins." For this baptism is not an isolated rite conferred "in the name of Jesus"; to be "baptized" means to "have completed a baptismal course." That is exactly what we saw in connection with John's baptism, and in particular its relationship to Essene institutions. In this sense the completion of baptism, with the Spirit, is the same as entry into the kingdom.

That is what was handed on by Paul once he had been turned round by the Spirit. As a messianist, he was already focused on the kingdom (to come). The new feature that he has come to realize is that by the Spirit, the Messiah (kingdom) is already here, which involves a new way of looking at baptism. This new feature goes together with the one we have just seen when Paul declares that he is "going to the Gentiles." In this picture Paul the ex-messianist now addresses a tiny, structured group connected with the baptism of John and does not seek a large audience or arouse dissensions. In what follows at Ephesus (Acts 19:8ff.), he will go from noisy meetings in the synagogue to long-term preaching before a little group of disciples. Thus, through a series of scenes that appear to be haphazard and isolated but in fact are characteristic, we can see taking shape what will finally be the Pauline doctrine, deeply rooted as it is in the tradition of which Paul made so much. The AT constantly anticipates the end result, but the WT allows us to reconstruct the steps that led to it.

One link in the chain is still missing, and that is the first of all: the discovery that this Messiah is none other than Jesus. That is what happened to Paul at Damascus. But from what we have already seen, it does not seem that the details of the life of Jesus played an important part at any of the stages of Paul's evolution. That is so for the Pauline kerygma, and it remains so for the Creed. This is a major difference between Paul and those who know "the things concerning Jesus," Apollos as well as the twelve at Ephesus.

III. THE BEGINNINGS OF THE MISSION

We shall conclude this chapter by glancing back through the narrative of the founding events in the Book of Acts, beginning with Paul's conversion and ending with Pentecost.

1. THE ROAD TO DAMASCUS

The "road to Damascus" runs close by the Sea of Galilee. In Galatians 1:12ff., Paul tells how he, the persecutor, had a direct revelation of Jesus Christ, then left for Arabia, and came back to Damascus. In 2 Corinthians 11:32, he recalls that at Damascus the ethnarch of King Aretas was guarding the city in order to arrest him. So there is a connection between persecution, revelation, and Damascus, which he fled before 39, the year of Aretas IV's death. Further, he says that he did not go up to Jerusalem until three years after his return to Damascus (Gal 1:18) and only then made the acquaintance of Cephas and James; he adds that no one in Judea knew him, but that a rumor went before him. For all that, he was very active and very visible, and if his activity was judged dangerous by the civil (non-Jewish) authorities of Damascus, it must have been because it stirred up trouble in society.

In order to work out what may have taken place, we need to consult all three narratives of Paul's conversion in Acts, which can provide details that are complementary. First, it is widely recognized that the insertion of Paul into the account of the stoning of Stephen is artificial. Then, the account of his conversion explains that there were "followers of the way" at Damascus (Acts 9:2; 22:4) and that he had obtained a commission from the high priest to arrest them and bring them to Jerusalem. These items locate Paul's activities in Jerusalem, where there were disciples, but they run up against two major difficulties. First, they formally contradict Paul's own statement that he was not personally known to the disciples in Jerusalem until three years later. Second, according to the general plan of Acts, there was as yet no mission farther afield than Samaria. We are surprised, then, to learn of these disciples at Damascus and find it hard to account for Paul's obvious interest in this city.

The Acts of the Apostles has, however, preserved some traces of the items provided by Galatians. According to Acts 9:26ff., Paul did indeed come to Jerusalem after leaving Damascus, but everyone was afraid of him. Even more interesting, it was Barnabas who introduced him to the apostles, as if he already knew him. But that is a secondary development, occasioned by the needs of the narrative: at Antioch, as we have seen, Barnabas hears that Saul is at Tarsus, so we are led to suppose that he knew him already. In any case, Barnabas is the one who puts Paul in touch with the mission originating in Jerusalem. In this way, Paul's activity in Damascus now appears less eccentric: Antioch is mid-way between Damascus and Tarsus, and he himself writes of time spent in Syria and Cilicia, which fits in very well (Gal 1:21).

At Damascus, Paul met disciples and was baptized (Acts 9:18). These were certainly Jewish and in some sense disciples of Jesus, but not messianists (like the disciples at Ephesus). In any case, his new message in the synagogues is characteristic (Acts 9:20a-22c): "He was proclaiming Jesus, that he is the Christ." He had already been a messianizing zealot. The fundamentally new feature is his identification of the Messiah as Jesus, giving rise to disturbances and anxieties among both Jews (Acts 9:23ff.) and Gentiles (2 Cor 11:32). The disciples who sent him off to Tarsus no doubt saved his life, but they were also removing someone who was dangerous for the community. In Acts 9:26 there is a trace of the fear that Paul inspired in the disciples. By the same token, that fear indicates that the disciples at Damascus formed a little group who were not in conflict with their Jewish neighbors. This peace is emphasized in Acts 9:31, that is, just after both Stephen and Paul have disappeared and Simon Magus has been neutralized—all of them linked with disorders.

We can see the sort of problem that someone like Barnabas had at Antioch and the risk he took in going to find someone like Paul. From much earlier in his career, Paul could have been called a *christianus* by the Romans, and if he had turned up at that stage in Jerusalem, he would certainly have aroused the greatest mistrust in the authorities, beginning with the high priest himself. Finally, there is no reason to think that at Damascus Paul would have shown any interest in Gentiles as such. Even his period in Arabia (see Gal 1:17) does not necessarily imply significant contact with Gentiles, since Jews had settled in the Nabatean kingdom. Paul only "turns to the Gentiles" much later, in circumstances that we have tried to discern. From the standpoint of his final position, he can, of course, see how the earlier stages of his career prepared for it and how the whole made sense under the direction of divine

Providence. In that perspective he can write to the Galatians (1:15f.): ". . . it pleased God, who set me aside from my mother's womb and called me through his grace, to reveal his Son in me, so that I might announce him among the nations."

2. EVENTS IN JERUSALEM

Perhaps the most remarkable feature of the early chapters of Acts is the stability of the community of disciples in Jerusalem. They are in no hurry to begin missionary activity, even among fellow Jews. There seems, in fact, to have been very little growth in numbers (here we should pay less attention to the "thousands" of 2:41 and 4:4 than to the remark of 5:13, according to which "no one else dared to join them, but the people praised them"). Instead, we are shown a small gathered community living its own way of life and occupied with its own affairs. Then things begin to move.

In Acts 3–5 we read a series of connected narratives beginning with the account of the paralyzed man raised up at the Beautiful Gate of the Temple by Peter and John "in the name of Jesus the Nazorean," leading to confrontations with the authorities. In the center (4:31) is the gift of the Spirit, as a confirmation of the power of God. The leading theme throughout is the resurrection of Jesus, proclaimed by the apostles and illustrated by the restoration of the sick man. The vocabulary is unambiguous: in 3:7a, Peter "raises up" the sick man, just as in 3:15 and 4:10 he declares that God has "raised up" Jesus from the dead. The healing is a sign expressing the reality of what is being proclaimed, which is given further confirmation by the Spirit. At this point Jesus is indeed "the Nazorean" and his name is powerful, but Peter does not declare that he is the Messiah. This is in striking contrast with the activity of Paul at Damascus and the anxieties that he arouses there.

Next Stephen, whose precise relationship to the group around Peter is not entirely clear, arouses violent popular indignation by preaching that "the Most High does not dwell in (houses) made by (human) hands" (7:48). Such a characterization of the Jerusalem Temple would have been resented at any time by those most attached to it, and especially by the priests in charge of it. If we are looking for a historical context in which Stephen's remarks would have aroused also the fury of the crowd, we might find it in the period when the emperor Caligula was moving to have his statue erected in the Temple.

According to Acts 8:1, a violent persecution drove a number of believers (but not the apostles) out of Jerusalem. This was the beginning of different missions, though no program had been drawn up in advance. This statement contains both facts and a thesis. The thesis is succinct and recurs throughout the Book of Acts, namely, that the mission progressed only thanks to persecutions. The first, directed against Jesus, allowed the Scriptures to be fulfilled by means of Judas and the Jewish authorities, who did not know what they were doing. The next caused the exit from Jerusalem toward the nations and eventually Rome. Obviously, nothing would have happened had it not been for the events concerning Stephen. In this sense Paul, even before his conversion, was already, without knowing it, helping the primitive community to develop.

The facts reinterpreted in this way were certainly less cut and dried: a persecution at Jerusalem, large or small in scale, connected no doubt with messianizing agitation but not easy to date (probably at the time of a pilgrimage). That does not rule out the possibility that the group of apostles had already left Jerusalem. A return to Galilee after the pilgrimage in which Jesus died is easy to imagine: the convergent testimony of Matthew, Mark, and John implies a mission beginning in Galilee. Paul's meetings with Cephas and James in Jerusalem (Gal 1:18ff.) do not change this conclusion, since they could have taken place during a pilgrimage (see Acts 20:16), which was certainly the best way to make sure of meeting people.

Throughout the Book of Acts, the cultural environment is close to that of the Essenes. The persistent allusions to "John's baptism" as the absolute origin of the whole movement launched by Jesus proves it, no less than the recurrent references to the breaking of the bread (without any particular link with Jesus' death). Onto this original stock two grafts were successfully implanted, represented respectively by Peter and by Paul, each acting independently but with authority: the former bringing together the resurrection of Jesus and healings of sick people, the latter renewing his disquieting messianic drive under the name of

Jesus but without any idea at first of a mission to the Gentiles. The growth of the community is infinitesimal in the first case and confused in the second, but at this stage everything stays within the Jewish world.

3. ASCENSION AND PENTECOST

It is becoming clearer that the development of NT Christianity occurred only gradually. The construction of Acts 1–2, which probably originated in the liturgy (with Pentecost on a Sunday), makes a synthesis that can be summed up in two phases. First, after the ascension the apostles' initial reflex is to wait passively for the return of the Messiah, who will come to establish his kingdom and set everything to rights; such an outlook—corresponding to James's position, which we have yet to see—is certainly not oriented toward any mission. Second, the angels bring everybody back to earth in order to wait for the Spirit; this opens up the perspective of a universal mission of conversion, whose success is necessarily distant. James is obviously absent from this phase, but the other two are much in evidence: Peter proclaiming the resurrection, and Paul pushing ahead with the development of the community and worrying the authorities.

However, it is not really a question of healing the sick, or of messianism properly so called. In other words, between the primitive figures of Peter and Paul and their final position in the frontispiece of Acts there have been other transformations, both connected with the resurrection of Jesus and with the Spirit. In the one case, the healing (raising up) of the sick has become a metaphor for the forgiveness of sin. In the other, the expectation of Jesus the Messiah has become the declaration that he has already returned and that the definitive kingdom has already come, as seen by the opening of all frontiers and the abolition of the line previously separating Jews from Gentiles.

Because Paul sees this kingdom of the Risen Christ (of the Messiah already returned) as a new creation, he naturally calls its founder "Lord." The narratives of Acts attribute Pauline features to Peter (preaching, visiting Gentiles) and Petrine features to Paul (healing; see Acts 19:11ff.). The figures of the two apostles end up by blending together, as the author intends, but without losing sight of communion with James, which is emphasized in the central episode of Acts, namely, the Jerusalem assembly (Acts 15). To that we must now turn our attention.

Chapter Five

James, Paul, and Peter

What is the link between the original environment from which Christianity came and the NT as we have it, that is to say, the heritage of Peter and Paul? The common ground is not well documented, but it is occupied by James and his successors in Judea. After the unplanned and uncertain beginnings, a distinction opens up among the adherents of Jesus between a main branch that is properly Jewish, or at least Jewish-centered and awaits his return as Messiah, and a branch that emerges as a new and unforeseeable phenomenon. This latter, coming forth with much hesitation from messianism properly so called and advocating communion with Gentiles ("neither Jews nor Greeks"), recognizes that Jesus is Lord, that is, that God has conferred on him "the Name that is above every name" (Phil 2:9). Despite their internal subdivisions, these two branches were characterized by contrasting attitudes toward the Law; either might at any moment receive new members, whether Jewish or Gentile in origin, but that does not affect their different indentities.

In this chapter we shall look at James and his heritage, the "Nazoreans," and then at their relations with other Jewish groups of similar type and with Christians of Petrine-Pauline type. These considerations will lead us to certain conclusions about the formation of the NT.

I. JAMES AT JERUSALEM

What was James's position? Apparent discrepancies between various NT texts have long been discussed. According to Galatians 2:11ff., Peter at Antioch was afraid of emissaries from James, who did not allow table fellowship with the uncircumcised. On the contrary, according to Acts 15:12ff., James seems to reply officially to Paul and Barnabas, who have come from Antioch, and to Peter on his return from Caesarea that circumcision is not necessary. We need to look more closely at these texts. This examination will show that at the beginning James accepted the conversion of Gentiles "to God" but kept them at a distance by excluding their circumcision. Such a position is in keeping with the messianic views that we shall find in his successors.

1. THE JERUSALEM DECREES

The account of the Jerusalem assembly includes some significant details (Acts 15:12-22). They are given here, in literal translation, indicating the chief variants of the WT (on the right hand side):

> (**15:**5) *Now there arose certain of the party of the Pharisees, who had become believers, saying that it was necessary to circumcise them and bid them observe the law of Moses.* (7a) *Now, a great discussion having come about, Peter rising up said . . .*
>
> (13b) *After they were silent, James replied saying: "Brethren, hear me.* (14) *Symeon has expounded how first God has visited in order to take from among the nations a people to his name.* (15) *The words of the prophets agree with that, since it is written:* (16) *'After that I will come and I will raise again the fallen tent of David. I will raise up its ruins and restore it,* (17) *so that the rest of humanity may seek the Lord* (WT: *God*), *as well as all the nations which have been consecrated to my name,' says the Lord who*

makes this (18) *since always known.*	*makes this.* (18) *Since always is known the Lord's work as his.*

> (19) *That is why I myself decide that it is not necessary to harass those of the Gentiles who turn to God.* (20) *Let us send to tell them to abstain*

from what has been polluted by idols,	*from what has been polluted by idols,*
from unchastity	*from unchastity*
from (anything) strangled	
and from blood.	*and from blood.*

(21) *Moses indeed from ancient times has
in each city*
*people who proclaim him in the synagogues, for he is read each
Sabbath.*

It is clear in verse 17 of the WT that for James it is a question
of Gentiles who are converted to God as attested by the Jews but
without any definite relationship with Jesus Christ; by contrast,
"the Lord" in the AT of the same verse allows a possible reference
to Jesus. This conversion of the Gentiles is the fulfilment of an eschatological prophecy (Amos 9:11ff.), where it is linked with the
reappearance of the posterity ("the fallen tent") of David, that is,
the resurrection of Jesus. However, the prophet does not predict
that these Gentiles will form one people with Israel. For James, too,
the arrival of Gentiles changes nothing in the status or nature of Judaism, for Moses is proclaimed each Sabbath in the synagogues.

The legal question to which James replies is therefore simple:
Should the nations that recognize God—a new fact—be integrated
into Israel or not, that is, concretely, subjected to the law of Moses
or not? The response, drawn from Amos, is: Clearly not; there is
no question of circumcising them, and so of integrating them into
the people. This response, with a Scriptural basis, reinforces the
reproach made to Peter on his return from seeing Cornelius, that
he went into his house and ate with him (Acts 11:3)—in other
words, that he had transgressed an essential barrier.

So, our text tells us, it is decided to transmit certain precepts to
these Gentiles. In their context in Acts, their meaning seems to be
that James raises no direct objection to Peter's action. He is ready to
accept table fellowship with uncircumcised folk on the condition
that they observe certain precepts derived from the prescriptions of
Leviticus 17–18, binding on Israelites and on foreign residents
alike and designed to avoid the major sources of impurity. But in
reality James says nothing of the sort: the frontiers are maintained.

Several conclusions follow. First, there is no longer any contradiction with Paul's statement of the situation in Galatians 2:11ff., according to which James refuses table fellowship with uncircumcised Gentiles, even if they have become believers. At the time of writing, Paul does not forget that he was once in communion with James (see Gal 2:9), but he has come a long way since then. Peter, for his part, has stayed in a more pragmatic position somewhere in between Paul and James.

How then would James have understood the "Jerusalem decrees"?

2. PRECEPTS FOR THE CHILDREN OF NOAH

We have already seen something of the God-fearers, those Gentiles who, in one way or another, were close to Jewish communities without, however, taking the step of formal conversion. Some of the decisive events in the "opening to the Gentiles" occurred among them. The rabbinic sources have, however, developed another approach to the Gentiles that is more consistent with their origins. Once the horizon has been expanded to take in the whole of the Jewish people and messianic hopes have been put off to an undetermined future, no missionary outlook is developed. On the contrary, the boundaries are made clear, and the intermediate category of "God-fearers" disappears, a development that may not be totally unconnected with the emergence of Christianity. All the same, in order to maintain a strictly monotheistic (and peaceable) perspective, the nations as a whole have to be given a place, without, however, engaging in properly missionary activity. That is the object of the "precepts for the children of Noah."

These precepts are given in various similar forms. The best known is in the Tosefta (*TAbZ* 8:4): "Seven commandments have been prescribed for the children of Noah; [they concern] judgments, blasphemy, idolatry, uncovering nakedness [forbidden unions], bloodshed, theft and living flesh [torn from a live animal]." The most notable feature of this list is that its global content, especially the five articles in the middle, form a sort of semi-Decalogue but that nothing in their formulation refers them expressly to the Decalogue (Ten Commandments) strictly so called. But we note here that the reference to these seven precepts is not the particular Covenant with Israel (Abraham) or its renewal (Sinai) or even Creation (implied in observance of the Sabbath), but Noah, that is to say, a very general Covenant between God and humanity as a whole. The difference is capital, because in this form there can no longer be any rivalry between Israel and the nations. By the same token, however, a God-fearer like Cornelius, close to the synagogue, no longer has a definite position or, more exactly, is sent back to his own nation.

These considerations bring us back directly to the Jerusalem assembly and the decrees of James. This is the moment to return to the question put by the Pharisees, before James's speech. The problem raised, which arises from Peter's stay with Cornelius in Caesarea, concerns contacts with Gentile converts. The response deals with Gentiles converted to God in general, without giving any very clear idea of what is meant by conversion; in fact, the response could equally well have applied to Cornelius before Peter's visit, since he had already begun to turn toward God. The real problem implied in all this is not in the first place contacts with these converts but their status.

We can now look at the content of James's speech. His opening statement uses a vocabulary characteristic of divine intervention (see Luke 1:68: "Blessed be the Lord, [. . .] for he has visited"), which governs the Covenant in general. However, he does not impose circumcision (the Covenant with Abraham) or the Ten Commandments (the Covenant at Sinai). In fact, the last prescription that he gives, to abstain from blood, refers directly to the Covenant with Noah (see Genesis 9:4ff., which prohibits both eating the blood of animals and shedding human blood). The prohibition of unchastity is also present in the story of Noah. According to Genesis 9:22, Ham has *uncovered* to his brothers the nakedness of their father, which earns him a curse. So there is implicitly a prohibition that can be developed into a complete body of laws governing sexual relations, since the expression "uncover the nakedness" precisely designates all the sexual prohibitions of Leviticus 18:5ff. Finally, the prohibition of the pollution of idols is simply a practical expression of monotheism, avoiding pagan feasts and rites, whereas Noah built an altar to YHWH (Gen 8:20).

From a Jewish point of view, monotheism is not a matter of opinions but of acts performed or avoided.

These remarks contain the answer to the obvious question about James's prescriptions. Why did he not forbid theft or murder (expressly) or the abandonment of children or covetousness, etc.? It is hardly likely that he was advocating moral laxity. Rather, we must conclude that in all these areas he was referring the addressees back to civil legislation, Roman or other, and so to the sanctions assigned there. From this angle he is close to the first of the Noachide precepts in the rabbinic list: the nations must have their own laws and judicial institutions. In other words, there is no need to be in communion with them, which would certainly imply circumcision, as required by the Pharisees.

To sum up, James associates Gentile converts neither with Abraham nor with Moses but with Noah. In so doing, he bases himself on an immemorial tradition that has no link with Jesus except by way of the restoration of the house of David, with an eschatological touch. Gently but firmly he keeps them at a distance from the Mosaic Covenant, which is maintained. Thus he is very close to the outlook of the rabbinic tradition on the Noachide laws. Finally, in later redactions of Acts, all these arrangements have simply been understood as facilitating relations between converts of different origins; they have only to be reinterpreted as if addressed to people converted to Jesus Christ, with the new significance of baptism and the Spirit.

James does not lay down anything about rites. Not only is circumcision missing but there is no mention of baptism, the breaking of the bread, or any other positive prescription relating to worship. Baptism is, however, in the background, not only in the case of Cornelius but also of the "Gentiles who have become believers," whom the Pharisees want to circumcise and whose faith is certainly expressed by visible acts, whether the baptismal process has yet been fully carried out or not. For them, these newcomers have in fact entered into the Covenant, and the question of circumcision then arises with a certain urgency. Confronted with this new reality, James says nothing. The apparent meaning of the discussion is that he accepts it, but the original meaning is that he rejects it. An undeniable divorce between Paul and James, foreseeable in its source, is thus concealed, and it is important to find out why.

In order to do this, we must examine the posterity left by James in Judea.

II. THE HERITAGE OF JAMES

What do we know about disciples of Jesus in Judea between James and the Bar Kokhba war? According to the historian Eusebius, until 135 all the bishops of Jerusalem were "Hebrews of ancient stock" (*Eccl. Hist.* 4.5.2-4), descended, like James, from the family of Jesus. Little is known about them, since they were distant from the circles that produced the NT. After 135 and Emperor Hadrian's expulsion of the Jews from Judea, including Jewish believers in Jesus, the Christians of Jerusalem (now renamed Aelia Capitolina) were attached to the diocese of Caesarea, which was of Western obedience.

1. THE JEWISH BISHOPS OF JERUSALEM

The principal item in the dossier is a list of fifteen bishops given by Eusebius (see the reference above). He states that he obtained his information from Hegesippus, a writer with a Jewish background contemporary with Trajan and Hadrian, but he makes clear that his source contained no chronological data. Other authors later on give various additional details, especially dates. In fact, it appears that the list in Eusebius is not a succession of bishops in the see of Jerusalem but a list of *episkopoi* who existed more or less at the same time, and it probably includes members of Jesus' family. They would have been in the same spirit as James, although it is difficult to establish a clear succession from him. The notion of a "diocese" of Jerusalem is not really suitable in this context, although that is precisely the fiction that Eusebius tries to introduce. Furthermore, we have no knowledge of multiple dioceses in Judea. In any case, it is certainly anachronistic to think in terms of territorial jurisdictions; it is better to ask what an *episkopos* (literally "overseer") might be and whether there could be more than one in the same region. Suffice it to say here that they were probably very similar to "overseers" of Essene groups qualified to pronounce on the admission or expulsion of members of the community.

Some confirmation of this hypothesis is provided by Eusebius himself, quoting Hegesippus (*Eccl. Hist.* 3.20.1-6), who reports that the grandsons of Jude, brother of the Lord (Matt 13:55), had been arrested as descendants of David on the order of Domitian, who feared the coming of a Messiah from the East. Brought before the emperor, they showed that they were simple folk who worked with their hands and had only a small amount of landed property. They were released as posing no danger and returned to "govern the churches." This narrative certainly includes some legendary elements, in particular the appearance before the emperor in Rome, but three facts stand out. First, these were country folk, small farmers or manual workers, which fits into the original Galilean environment, far from towns. Next, that they were related to the Lord qualified them to be heads of communities, as with James; although their function is not named, it corresponds well to that of "bishops" in the sense of the list of Hegesippus. Finally, there are several communities, and there is no definite link with Jerusalem.

2. THE NAZOREANS

The term "Nazorean(s)" occurs many times in the NT (sometimes in the form "Nazarene"), where it appears to be applicable both to Jesus personally and to others. It is also the name of a "Jewish-Christian" sect known to Epiphanius (*Panarion* 29) and to other early Christian writers. Finally, it is still the term by which Christians are known in various Semitic languages. What is the connection between these uses? What does the term originally mean? Simply "from Nazareth"? We shall see that the Nazoreans are at once "the brothers of Jesus" and the posterity of James.

The epithet "Nazorean" is applied several times to Jesus himself. There are two instances in Matthew. In 2:23, the town of Nazareth, where Joseph and his family go to live, is related to an unidentified verse taken from "the prophets" and applied to Jesus: "He will be called a Nazorean." In Matthew 26:69, 71, two serving women in succession ask Peter if he was with Jesus the Galilean, then with Jesus the Nazorean; the two expressions evidently have much the same meaning. Equally obviously, they both have a geographical meaning. However, as we have seen (chap. 3, §I.2), the term "Galileans" also designates zealots, which may not be irrelevant to Peter's own origins, and "Nazorean" seems to mean more than "from Nazareth," as the false quotation of Matthew 2:23 shows. (Nazareth may well have begun as a settlement of Nazoreans.) In Luke's Gospel there is only one instance: in 18:37 the blind beggar at Jericho is told that "Jesus the Nazorean is passing by" and cries out, "Jesus, Son of David, have pity on me." So the name is associated here with descent from David, as we have seen in connection with James's succession.

In Acts, to be seen here as a continuation of Luke, the term appears six times to designate Jesus: in 2:22; 3:6; 4:10; 6:14; 22:8; 26:9. To these references should be added a mention of Jesus' disciples on the occasion of Paul's trial (Acts 24:5), where he is accused by an advocate appearing for the high priest of stirring up trouble "in our nation and in the entire world, being a leader of the sect of Nazoreans." The movement is here called a "sect," like the Sadducees (Acts 5:17) or the Pharisees (15:5); it is obviously a Jewish movement. Paul in reply does not say he is a Nazorean, but disputes the term "sect" and states that he is a follower of the Way, at the same time protesting his peaceful conduct.

So there is something of a gap between the two views of Paul. From the Jewish side he is regarded as a Nazorean; he himself does not really deny this but insists on his fidelity to the Law and the Prophets. The term seems to present a danger, but what and for whom? It is applied to Jesus and to his disciples, which is unique—all other titles of Jesus are proper to him. What is more, it is generally given by Jews who are outside the group of disciples, except in the case of Peter in Acts, who insists on the name "Jesus the Nazorean."

That brings us to the testimony of John. The charge written by Pilate had "Jesus the Nazorean, the king of the Jews" (John 19:19). Afterward the high priests contested the second part of the inscription but not the first: he was indeed "Jesus the Nazorean," whom they had earlier sent to find (John 18:5, 7). So he was known by this name, even though he never calls himself by it. In this instance, as before, the title carries overtones of kingship or at least of power of some kind.

Thus we have found several indications that the name goes back to Jesus, but we still need to find out if it is favorable or not. In the case of the charge on the cross, it may serve to identify Jesus or to give the reason for his condemnation, made explicit as a claim to kingship. However, the "Jewish-Christians" known to Epiphanius, who called themselves Nazoreans and were presumably not innovating, and the use of the title by Peter (before any meeting with Gentiles), prevent us from seeing it as a mere nickname given by opponents. It must come from the group surrounding Jesus. On the other hand, the title is clearly residual in the NT as we have it, which often seeks to neutralize it by emphasizing the geographical reference (Jesus "the Nazarene"), which is the one generally perceived by translators (Jesus "of Nazareth"). The simplest hypothesis is to see this eclipse as the sign of an intention, at the moment of the final redaction, to keep a safe distance from the Nazoreans.

To throw light both on the meaning of the title and the reservations shown toward it, we need only bring together Epiphanius's Nazoreans, who come from Jerusalem, and James's successors, reported by Hegesippus, who can boast Davidic descent and give rise to suspicions on the part of the Romans. It is clear that James and his successors are equally descendants of David and can bear the same title, and by extension their partisans. In other words, we come back to the marked kinship usually admitted between "Nazoreans" *(nosrim)* and the shoot *(neser)* springing from the root of Jesse, father of David (Isa 11:1). There may well be also an allusion to the verb *nasar,* "to observe, watch," allowing both for the connotation of "observing" the Covenant and "watching" for the signs of the Messiah.

Thus we have a group based, at least notionally, on descent from David; from them the Messiah will come. Jesus was a Nazorean, and so were his "brothers." The victorious Messiah is not, however, identified as any of the Nazoreans already known, not even as Jesus in his lifetime, but he is awaited from among them, in the form of the return of this same Jesus or a successor, who will then be recognized as Messiah or king. This enables us to understand how it was that Jesus and his successors bore the same title and that descent from David was followed with such extreme attention; what Hegesippus and Eusebius have to say on this point should not be dismissed as fantasy. Another consequence is that the identification of Jesus, and of him alone, as Messiah should be regarded as a further development in the community. In the meantime, after Jesus' ascension into heaven, James and the other Nazoreans await the moment when God will send the foreordained Messiah (see Acts 3:20).

3. JAMES'S ECLIPSE AND RETURN TO FAVOR

In two places Eusebius mentions that the Christians of Judea were circumcised: once when he records the accession of Justus (*Eccl. Hist.* 3.35), and later, when he gives the list already discussed, he adds that the Church of Jerusalem as a whole was formed of believing Hebrews (4.5.2). This detail is instructive. Not only were they of Jewish origin, but even more they were circumcised and observant. In other words, the information given by Eusebius, that the Judean group associated with James was formed of observant Jews, is perfectly consistent. Furthermore, the continuing rumor that James and his successors were of David's stock is a messianic symptom that is strictly Jewish. In that case, the difficulty of establishing a clear succession from James raises two problems that are connected: Why is there no significant information about the immediate successors of James? And, at the same time, why is Eusebius so careful to emphasize the legitimacy of the Church of Jerusalem, despite what seems to have been something of an eclipse? The question becomes all the more acute in the light of Eusebius's extreme mistrust of any kind of heresy and of Judaism; he does not deal kindly with the Ebionites (*Eccl. Hist.* 3.27), who have no known link with James. We might go so far as to allow that for him the successors of James constituted an extinct branch and were not a problem for his own time.

It is in fact understandable that there should not have been much information available about James and his immediate successors and their followers: the problems with the Judaizers at

Antioch or Corinth were enough to explain why groups of a Pauline type, dominant in the publication of the NT, kept their distance, since contact was impossible. We can even understand perfectly well why such groups delayed a long time before giving final form to the Gospels, that is, to biographies of Jesus, which originated in Jewish circles. But then, why this new-found interest in the Jewish bishops of Jerusalem at the time of Trajan and Hadrian? It seems to imply some contact at a later stage, on the occasion of events that were sufficiently important to relegate ancient quarrels to the past.

Different convergent facts enable us to form a hypothesis. First, under Trajan and Hadrian there was a climate of persecution, both of Jews and of Christians. Then, remarkably, the rabbinic sources begin to concern themselves with "sectaries" *(minim),* including *noṣrim,* only in the time of Gamaliel II, that is after 90, which brings us close to Trajan and Hadrian and also to Hegesippus's "bishops." In other words, at a certain moment the Jewish disciples of Jesus were regarded as having changed sides. The simplest conclusion is that up till then, the successors of James were hardly distinguishable from other fraternities. This category certainly contained many currents, some of them more or less messianic.

The event that brought Jewish believers in Jesus closer to Pauline Christians could well have been persecution. But more is needed to explain a rejection by other Jews, culminating in Bar Kokhba's persecution of "Christians" during the war (Justin, *First Apology* 31.6). At some previous point, communication between these groups must have occurred. We shall see that one form that it took was the circulation of written texts.

III. TANNAITES AND NAZOREANS

Officially, for the pre-Constantinian Jewish sources, Christianity does not exist, that is to say, is not a significant event in the history of Judaism. This view is in agreement with a traditional outlook, according to which the Mishnah is supposed to issue from an environment representing the whole people, and so is the natural heir to the totality of traditions from before the two destructions of 70 and 135. The symmetrical view, with which the NT is imbued, consists in regarding the Christians as the true Israel. Underlying all this are more or less muted polemics. In fact, on the Jewish side there are various signs of positions taken with regard to Christianity at an early stage; certain questions were even sufficiently important to have played an appreciable role in the development of the rabbinic system.

1. TRACES OF POLEMICS

Rabbinic Judaism shows great mistrust of all manifestations of messianism, even of its most obscure symbols. Indeed the rabbinic tradition distances itself from all apocalyptic and eschatological speculations on salvation in order to concentrate on the sanctification of daily life. This reaction is too general to be due simply to a single event, no matter how traumatic, such as the failure of Bar Kokhba. It seems to betray an abiding danger that was at the same time a temptation. In the second century the Tannaites, the transmitters of the rabbinic tradition, were creative also in the biblical field. One result was to canonize a particular form of the Hebrew text of the Bible (the "Massoretic Text" = MT); correspondingly, a new Greek translation (that of Aquila) appeared, which was closer to the MT than the Septuagint, which had become the Bible of the Christians. One of the mechanisms at work was clearly the desire to keep Christianity at a distance, and in the first place those Christians who were more aware of messianism in the Jewish sense.

Another example of the same mechanism is the emphasis in rabbinic Judaism on 613 precepts all of equal weight; in this way the rabbinic tradition makes it impossible to center the Covenant on a single precept. To get a clearer idea of what is at stake, let us return a moment to the fraternities (see above, chap. 3, §V.1). The *ḥaber* is defined as one who eats in a state of Levitical purity. That does not mean that he does not observe the other commandments, but only that for him they all converge on one precept that brings the rest together. The same could be said of the Essenes: to take part in the "purity," the community meal, presupposes not only the completion

of the baptismal course but also faithful observance of the whole
Law, since any violation that is picked up entails a certain degree of
impurity, separating the offender for a shorter or longer time from
the meal. The same is true in Christianity, of all periods, with its procedures of access to the Eucharist and excommunication.

These elements coalesce around the term "sectarians" *(minim)*,
which enters into the sources from the time of Gamaliel II's reorganization at Yavneh. We recall that his enterprise was to form a comprehensive Judaism that could embrace the people as a whole.
Therefore membership of the Jewish nation, with circumcision as
the sign of the Covenant, was all-important; correspondingly, there
was no longer a place within Judaism for the exclusive features of
the fraternities or of the Essene communities. So the banishment of
the *minim*—a term that referred to the disciples of Jesus, though not
only to them—was a logical consequence. In addition, the Nazoreans (the *noṣrim* of the rabbinic sources) had become, from a Jewish
point of view, contaminated with Christianity of a Pauline type. The
barrier between Jew and Gentile was becoming dangerously porous.

2. THE DANGER OF CHRISTIANITY

The moves indicated above would seem to be reactions to an
active Christian proselytism affecting circles close to those that
were defining emergent rabbinic Judaism. We can get some idea
of what may have been involved by considering the successive attitudes of the rabbis to the Greek and Aramaic (Syriac) languages.

There is plenty of evidence that the Greek language was used
and well regarded in (proto-)rabbinical circles in the first century
and again in the third. In between, however, it fell out of favor.
This sudden fear of Greek can be explained by a new contact between Jewish believers in Jesus and Christians of another type. We
can infer that Gentile Christian missionaries began to make their
appearance at the end of Trajan's reign or the beginning of
Hadrian's, at the same time as the zealot spirit was on the rise once
more among the Jews; they may even have contributed toward that
rise. These Christians probably came from Rome and brought with
them some books in Greek, in more or less published form. We
have seen that Justin, with his *Memoirs of the Apostles,* attests a

first stage in which there were authoritative texts, even if they had not yet been formally published (chap. 1, §I.1).

At this point the question of the circulation of texts must be broadened and seen as going in both directions. It may have been at this moment that the epistles of James and Jude, of Jewish type, were brought into the collection that was in the process of becoming the NT; that would agree with the fact that their canonicity was under discussion until the third century. Similarly, the *Gospel of the Hebrews* mentioned by Eusebius (*Eccl. Hist.* 3.27.4) may have some connection with a properly Jewish form of Matthew. It is difficult to be more precise about the circumstances of these new exchanges under Trajan and Hadrian; we can only suppose that they did not happen overnight. We should also bear in mind that Greek was common to all. These exchanges of texts, which were not published but were of apostolic authority, would not have taken place without creating some tensions between those who accepted and those who rejected them. If there were doubts in Gentile circles about the epistles of James and Jude, it is very probable that there were also corresponding hesitations over the texts newly arrived in Judea.

Later, after 200, the patriarch Judah, the editor of the Mishnah, accepted Greek with honor but showed mistrust of Aramaic. The center of activity is now Galilee, around the Lake. This gives a clue to understanding why the danger from Christianity is no longer connected with Greek but with Syriac. The spread of Christianity eastward, to eastern Syria and Mesopotamia, is not well documented. But even if Christianity existed in these regions well before 200, the spread of Christian texts, whether the Syriac NT translated from the recently canonized Greek or even only a Gospel harmony such as the *Diatessaron* of Tatian, belongs to this period.

By the end of the second century, there was at Edessa in Upper Mesopotamia a sizeable Christian community that acknowledged its dependence on Antioch, cradle of all the Eastern churches that adopted the NT and center from which Christianity progressively reached the interior of Syria (Damascus, Palmyra) and Parthia/Persia (Seleucia-Ctesiphon). Syriac, both the language and the writing, originated as that branch of eastern Aramaic proper to the region of Edessa and is very close to the Aramaic of the Talmud.

The conclusion is simple: the Aramaic banished by Judah was really Syriac. His intention was to protect his community against a threat that was connected with texts in Aramaic, whose circulation was certainly due to a new missionary wave, but coming this time from Damascus and Edessa. In fact, the rejection of Syriac was only temporary. Mistrust of Greek also disappeared. This implies that the Greek-speaking churches, even those nearby (Caesarea Maritima), had taken a position quite independent of Judaism (after 135) and that the missionary effort had changed direction. Thus the measures taken with regard to Syriac and Greek are strictly parallel, and both appear to have been taken, at different times, for the same reason.

To sum up, it seems that the circles that produced the Mishnah had to position themselves pragmatically with regard to the ways Christianity was developing. For our purposes this has a twofold importance. First, these problems concerning Jewish believers throw light on the original environment of Jesus' disciples and fill out what we saw earlier in chapters 2 and 3. Second, the way to use the earliest rabbinic sources can be refined. At first there were very clear areas of kinship with the environment of primitive Christianity; then measures were taken to keep a distance between the two; finally, these measures were hidden by later developments, at the moment when the fraternities broadened their horizon to include the people as a whole. The idea behind these moves was presumably to show that the appearance of Christianity was not a notable event in the history of Judaism but only a very lateral, if unfortunate, incident.

IV. THE FORMATION OF THE NEW TESTAMENT

The general purpose of our study has been to depict the environment in which Christianity began by defining its characteristic institutions. Already an examination of Christian and Jewish literary sources has led us to give great importance to events and texts of the second century. By contrast, evidence from the first century is rarely direct and has in most cases been transmitted through successive redactions over a period of more than a hundred years.

These facts have two consequences that justify the procedure that has been followed. First, the distinction between historical facts and customs is of the first importance. Second, even if oral transmission was long dominant, Christians possessed collections of notes on the life of Jesus, which no doubt enjoyed apostolic authority. Thanks to the distinction that we established at the outset between composition or redaction and publication, we can see how such collections could circulate and evolve. There is no decisive reason to suppose that formal, definitive publication took place all at once. Since the basic act of written publication is to make a copy (or translation), it is natural to imagine rather successive editions, from which in turn copies were made, with resulting contaminations, then revisions, etc. As far as the NT is concerned, the idea of a written, published canon, that is, an authoritative selection, emerges in various forms between Justin and Irenaeus, but always in the West, a fact that deserves to be noticed. We do not know precisely what circumstances, that is, what conflicts of authority, led to the production of these fixed lists. It is reasonable, however, to think that in any case, with the passage of time, such collections must have been changed less and less as the apostolic traditions became ever more ancient and so venerable.

In the introductory chapter we saw that the publication of the Gospels, that is, biographies of Jesus, came about only quite late. Closely related to this is the fact that Paul's letters, the Roman Creed, and, more generally, a whole stream of early Christianity speak of Jesus only as crucified and risen and not as healer, teacher, or Messiah. The case of the Jewish believers, with their *Gospel of the Hebrews,* allows us to press the question more closely. In the sources they are divided into two branches, but it is hard to know at this stage if they were really distinct. In one camp are James and his successors. Until they disappear after Bar Kokhba, they are revered as "sons of David" and await the return of Jesus as Messiah. In the other are the much-disparaged "Jewish-Christians," including the "Nazoreans," on whom Jerome passes the harsh judgment that had already become traditional: "Since they wish to be both Jews and Christians, they are neither one nor the other." Their fate was indeed hard: excluded both by emerging rabbinic Judaism and by emerging NT Christianity.

1. THE NAZOREANS AND THE GOSPELS

Since the canonical gospels are biographies of Jesus, it is natural to look there for traces of the original environment and, in the background, signs of rabbinical condemnations. The Gospels, in fact, distance themselves somewhat from symptoms of Nazoreanism, but preserve traces of it. The interplay already noted between the use of the term "Nazorean" and the apparently synonymous "Nazarene" points to ancient debates about the Davidic descent of Jesus, and especially about the meaning of that descent, in which the Nazorean element has been watered down as much as possible. There are other traces of the same debate. Matthew and Luke, with their genealogies and Jesus' birth at Bethlehem, affirm his Davidic ancestry without using the term "Nazorean" in this context. John 7:41f. expressly denies it, emphasizing that Jesus came from Galilee (see also 1:45ff.), and refuses to associate Jesus' messianic identity in any way with descent from David: "When the Messiah comes, no one will know where he is from" (John 7:27). In Revelation 5:5 and 22:16, Jesus calls himself "the root and the posterity of David," with a transparent allusion to Isaiah 11:10 ("the root of Jesse") but avoiding verse 1, which has exactly the same meaning but lends itself to a more explicitly "Nazorean" coloring.

The conflicts with the Jews in the NT can now be put in perspective. Take first the Johannine community. Recent studies of John have shown that this Gospel is more Jewish than used to be thought and that it needs to be read on two levels: at the same time as it tells and reinterprets the story of Jesus, it presents also the later story of the Johannine Christians. In particular, fear of the Jews and exclusion from the synagogue in John 9:22 (as well as the expulsions foretold in 16:2) do not concern Jesus' own days but later conflicts, at a moment when "among the leaders themselves, many had come to believe in him, but, because of the Pharisees, they did not dare to confess him, for fear of being excluded from the synagogue" (John 12:42).

The final editorial touch of this Gospel is not Nazorean and is even opposed to this tendency. Thus we see weakening of messianic and Davidic shades of meaning; insistence on the resurrection, the Spirit (20:21 ff.), and the non-messianic universal mission (John 4:35ff., 12:19ff.). If these few aspects are omitted, however, the environment in which the Fourth Gospel originated emerges as clearly Nazorean and in conflict with the Jews, especially the Pharisees. These Jewish adversaries belong to circles that are close and doubtless very active, and they are not the people as a whole or the authorities of Jerusalem. Taking into account what has already been said about the similar origins of the first Tannaites and of the disciples of Jesus, the conclusion is self-evident: this later conflict is none other than the struggle against the *minim,* attested by the rabbinic sources, after 90 and in relation with Gamaliel II's reorganization.

Similar remarks can be made for the other Gospels. Thus the fundamental question discussed by Matthew is of a sectarian type: Which is the true Israel? The parables of the kingdom include menacing scenes in which the legitimate heirs are dispossessed; it is a family quarrel. There, too, a twofold reading has to be made. On one level the Gospel tells the traditional story of Jesus, continuing that of John the Baptist and connected, as we have seen, with groups of reformers of Essene type. Superimposed on this is the growing hostility of Israel toward Jesus' disciples, a later stage that followed a calmer period represented by Matthew 17–20, which is dominated by training for mission. At the end there is a final split. Among the Jews, it is told "until this day" that the body of Jesus was smuggled away during the night (28:12ff.).

Likewise, to proclaim the resurrection would be "worse than the first imposture," say the high priests and the Pharisees. The association of these two groups is an anachronism, since historically they were opposed. The risen Jesus sends out his disciples to all nations and declares that he will be with them until the end of time (Matt 28:16ff.). But that is not really messianism, since here Jesus occupies the place of the Paraclete in John or the Spirit in Acts, and all the other titles fall into second place. In other words, the eventual conflict of the community with the Pharisees, long after Jesus, is superimposed on the condemnation of Jesus by the authorities, then rebounds as a mission to the Gentiles, or more exactly to the whole world.

This ultimate conflict, expressed very aggressively, strongly resembles the crisis of the *minim;* it is a properly Jewish problem, still closely bound up with a form of messianism. On the other hand, the universal mission opens up another horizon, according to which it is precisely thanks to this conflict that such a mission could develop, by moving out of a strictly Jewish messianism. That is the theory expressed in Romans 11:11ff.: "Thanks to their [the Jews'] stumbling, the Gentiles have access to salvation."

It is hard to pin down the precise stages in the formation of our Gospels, but the final crisis seems to have had a twofold dimension, corresponding to two phases of literary composition. First, the Jewish believers are rejected by the dominant forces in Judaism as *minim* at the same time as a conjunction is brought about with groups of Pauline type. Finally, the fading out of the title "Nazorean" points to an estrangement from those Jewish believers who refused this conjunction. Such an outline also shows a further channel by which a biography of Jesus could have circulated and then been transformed.

2. LUKE–ACTS

In the opening chapters of Luke's Gospel, the benediction uttered by Symeon on seeing Jesus is unambiguous: "Light to enlighten the Gentiles, and glory of Israel your people" (2:32). However, as early as the inaugural sermon at Nazara/Nazareth (4:16ff.), the congregation is at first enthusiastic, then rejects Jesus and wants to stone him when he cites biblical references to salvation brought to the Gentiles. Similarly, Paul's inaugural sermon at Antioch of Pisidia, also in a synagogue, at first arouses enthusiasm (Acts 13:42 ff.), but on the following Sabbath the Jews oppose him and unleash a persecution (Acts 13:45, 50). In both cases the rejection is modeled on the Deuteronomic figure of the rejected prophet, who is striving to save Israel from itself. That is also the final scene in Acts 28:26ff., where Paul at Rome quotes Isaiah 6:9-10 to the Jews who are divided among themselves ("For the heart of this people has grown dull"), but at the same time proclaims a hope. Two conflicts in which the mission to the Gentiles plays a decisive role have been superimposed: first opposition to Jesus, then opposition to Paul and his companions.

Putting these two distinct historical moments in parallel is, however, a deliberate literary effect, as several indications show. For one thing, the Pharisees are represented as opponents from the beginning (Luke 6:2ff.), but they are not there at the passion (Luke 22–23); then they defend the apostles (Acts 5:33ff.; 22:3; 23:1-10), and at the end Paul says he is one of them (Acts 23:6). The problem of Jewish opposition (James, Pharisees) to the abandoning of the Law by Jewish converts is entirely played down. The resulting effect is twofold: on the one hand, Paul and James are represented as united, while "the Jews" are divided; on the other hand, the Christians are finally the true Pharisees, that is, the true Israel.

3. TOWARD A CANON

Luke's double work is remarkable for suggesting a synthesis of the positions of Peter, Paul, and James. The credit given there to the Jewish tendency (James, Peter) suggests that the chief material for Luke's Gospel and for the first half of Acts originated in those quarters. These traditions have, however, been integrated into a universalist perspective that is properly Pauline. The constant model of interpretation is the sequence of death-resurrection in fulfillment of the Scriptures.

The conjunction of Peter, Paul, and James is presented dramatically in the central scene of Acts 15, the Jerusalem assembly. In this chapter we have realized something of the difficulty of reconciling the scene in Acts historically with Paul's accounts in Galatians 2. Nevertheless, it is worth noting that Paul himself remembers an agreement concerning the mission between himself and the "columns" of Jerusalem, James, Cephas, and John (see Gal 2:9). So Luke's synthesis is not entirely without historical foundations.

The names just mentioned—Paul, James, Cephas, and John— represent the bulk of the writings that are found in the canonical NT, taking Cephas/Peter to represent the Synoptic Gospels as well as the two epistles bearing his name. Their voices are not unanimous, in the sense of all saying exactly the same thing in the same way. On the other hand, the effect of bringing them into a canon, in the sense of a defined list, is to resolve discords into a harmony, or, perhaps more aptly, to interpret them in accordance with a canon, in the sense of a rule. That rule is the agreement of Peter and Paul. In other words, the life of Jesus and the structures inherited from the original environment are to be interpreted in the light of the proclamation that his death and resurrection work salvation here and now. Symbolically, the canon is stated in the words of Tertullian, that Peter and Paul "poured forth all their doctrine with their blood" (*Prescription* 36). Once again, "the blood of martyrs is the seed of Christians." In the same statement Tertullian refers to the Church of Rome: it is indeed to Rome that we should look for the canon (in both senses of the word) and for the Lucan synthesis.

The formation of the New Testament obviously supposes the circulation of texts. What were the channels of communication among the different communities? The principal cities of the empire were Rome, Alexandria, and Antioch, with excellent communications among them. The paths taken by Peter and Paul, in the redaction of Acts, led to Rome, with a major halt at Antioch, where the name of Christians was given to the disciples and where the crisis arising from the mission to the Gentiles took place, reinterpreted as having provoked the Jerusalem assembly. By contrast, Alexandria is deliberately bypassed, as if it had not been possible to bring that city into the harmonious outlook of Acts.

Against the background of communications in the Roman world there stands out what could be called a second axis, one end of which is in Judea and Galilee and the other in Asia Minor, with an extension to Achaia (Corinth). This axis is illustrated by the Fourth Gospel. On the one hand, John shows a precise acquaintance with the realities of Palestine, Samaritans, John the Baptist, etc., and gives a chronology for Jesus that is more realistic than those in the Synoptics. On the other hand, the tradition reported by Irenaeus (*Against the Heresies* 3.1.1) places this Gospel's origin at Ephesus, the most venerable city of the province of Asia, the region also indicated for the Johannine tradition by the Book of Revelation. However, the appendix of John 21, Johannine in style and centered on Peter, emphasizes an undeniable link with Rome.

4. FINAL REMARKS

In NT Christianity the agreement of Peter and Paul is not exclusive. Notably, it does not exclude James but includes him, along with Jude, who is closely related to him (as also to the Second Epistle of Peter). The canon also includes John, who represents other currents. The significance of founding NT Christianity on the agreement of Peter and Paul but not excluding James can be seen more clearly when it is contrasted with the canon supposed by the Pseudo-Clementine literature, that is, the agreement of Peter and James and excluding Paul, who is regarded as a traitor.

When disciples of Jesus turned to the Gentiles, it was from every point of view a major event. Such a development could not have been foreseen at the outset, and it entailed a long series of difficulties, since the primitive community was by nature observant and saw itself at the center of the tradition of Israel. Fairly rapidly a gap widened between Paul and James, while Peter held a pragmatic position in between. The position of Peter, striving to promote a quasi-impossible synthesis, stands out more clearly.

In this context mention should also be made of another quite different figure, venerated by tradition, in the person of Mary. In Acts 1:14 Mary, the mother of Jesus, is placed at the point of conjunction between the "heirs," who find themselves divided into two camps that later history shows to have been in rivalry (and see Matt 12:46-50 par.): on the one hand "his brothers," and on the other "the disciples," all, however, "persevering in prayer with some women." A similar synthesis is suggested by John when he tells how the dying Jesus confided his mother to the disciple whom he loved (19:25-27).

We need now to return to consideration of the Covenant and its central symbols, in order to gain greater clarity about what was traditional and what was new in Christianity.

Chapter Six

The Covenant

The term *christiani* is of Roman origin. We have seen how it was grafted onto some of Jesus' disciples from the time of the disturbances over Caligula's statue. Our search for the origins of Christianity is not yet closed, however, for we have to see why this graft "took," and therefore, following our method, find a link with rites and customs.

The original Jewish-Christian environment, represented by James, remained the trunk onto which the different grafts were implanted. The resulting synthesis is depicted by the scene of Pentecost in Acts 2, which features a quasi-Pauline Christianity under the leadership of Peter less than two months after the death of Jesus. That is extremely quick. In reality, the various episodes retold in Acts are worked into a connected and coherent whole by being put under the sign of the Spirit. On the other hand, the whole process is started up in the setting of a Pentecost that has become the feast of the Spirit, that is, of the risen Jesus now alive and active in the world.

For Pentecost to have attracted such a vast synthesis, the feast must already have had enough substance, in terms of distinctive rites with precise meanings. In our study of Jesus' Last Supper, we saw that the elements of bread and wine convey a reference to Pentecost as a feast of first fruits and of the Covenant (chap. 2, §II.3). In the Synoptic Gospels, Jesus foresees his own death, which represents the failure of a political messianism. At the same time he suspends the celebration of Passover until a moment as yet undefined, when the kingdom will finally come. In other words, Passover was effaced from the liturgical rhythm, while Pentecost was promoted as the Church's feast between the two Passovers, past and future, with the death of Jesus reinterpreted as the sacrifice suitable for renewing the Covenant.

I. PASSOVER

Passover has nevertheless left a strong imprint in the NT and serves as a point of reference for the specifically Christian celebration of Easter.

1. THE PASCHAL LAMB

One trace of Passover with which Christians are very familiar, both from the Gospels and from the liturgy, is the use of the expression "the Lamb of God" for Jesus. What is the precise point of the title? Justin Martyr tells us what the paschal lamb looked like: "When the lamb is roasted, it is arranged in such a way as to represent the cross: a spit goes right through it from the lower limbs to the head, another spit is at the shoulder, to which the hooves are fastened" (*Dialogue with Tryphon* 40.3; see Melito of Sardis, fr. 9). This description, which is not drawn from the Bible, may well show the influence of Christian symbolism, but it must have been close enough to actual Jewish custom for it to have made some sense to the Jew Tryphon, with whom Justin is in debate.

The Jewish custom referred to by Justin is attested by rabbinic sources, whose interpretation requires some technical specifications. First, according to Exodus 12:9, the lamb must be "neither raw nor boiled, but roasted over the fire." Further, according to the Mishnah (*MPes* 7:1), the lamb is to be roasted on a spit of dry wood. Damp wood gives off steam, with an effect similar to that of boiling, whereas a metal spit heats up in the fire and so would play a part in cooking the meat. The intestines pose a further problem: contained within the body, they would be cooked as in a pot and not roasted directly over the fire. For this reason Rabbi Aqiba requires them to be fastened on another branch fixed to the hooves so that they can be outside the carcass. In other words, there has to be a second, transverse spit forming a cross with the first.

The specifically culinary explanation converges with Justin's overall description. Jesus is very simply identified with the paschal lamb, giving an eloquent symbolism to the cross and emphasizing the wood. That also explains, by the way, why the Christian cross has four branches, whereas a gallows, normally shaped like a T, has only three. Whatever the exact shape of the instrument of execution, the symbolism of the lamb on a cross is simple and significant.

This Christian confiscation—from a Jewish point of view—of the paschal lamb may help to explain its disappearance from the Jewish Passover *seder.* This is celebrated in the same way, without the lamb, everywhere, even in Jerusalem. By contrast, the Samaritans still continue to celebrate the biblical rite with the lamb (see Exod 12) on their sacred mountain Gerizim, even though no temple has stood there since the end of the second century B.C. In fact Gamaliel II, well after the destruction of the Jerusalem Temple, was still roasting the paschal lamb, but on a grid (*MPes* 7:2), thereby avoiding the symbolism of the cross. The current rite, without the lamb, was established in its essentials before 200 A.D., and so precisely in the period when rabbinic Judaism was marking itself off from Christianity. It is therefore of interest to note that the rabbinic *seder* also lacks any properly messianic element, even though Jewish tradition testifies eloquently to the messianic dimension of the feast.

2. PASSOVER AND EASTER

The Passover on 14 Nisan was in fact observed by certain Christians in Asia Minor in the second century. They are known as "Quartodecimans," from the Latin word for "fourteen." We can well suppose that the "Nazoreans" in Judea similarly observed the Passover.

The Quartodeciman rite can be reconstructed as follows. It took place during the night of 14 to 15 Nisan, until three o'clock in the morning. During the Jewish celebration of Passover, the Quartodecimans kept a fast on behalf of their Jewish brethren who did not believe in Jesus; it was only then, around midnight, that the joyful feast began. At the same time, the ritual was apparently the same; it included commentary on the Passover narrative of the deliverance from Egypt (Exod 12), insisting on the fact that the lamb designates Christ, as we find in Melito of Sardis's *Paschal Sermon.* In accordance with the Jewish expectation that the Messiah would come on the night of Passover, they were hoping for the Parousia in the middle of the night, as at the Exodus. The principal moment of the feast was then the *agapē* and the Eucharist, which broke the fast.

The paschal fast is a matter of prime importance and was the occasion, around 191, of a memorable controversy (see Eusebius, *Eccl. Hist.* 5.23-24). For in all other churches, it continued until the "day of the resurrection," the Sunday. The bishops in the Quartodeciman camp, led by Polycrates, bishop of Ephesus, defended their tradition as apostolic, with the authority of John and Philip, as well as that of Polycarp of Smyrna. The spokesman for the opposite camp, which was in the majority, was Victor, bishop of Rome, who had no argument to offer except that of authority; apparently, if Irenaeus had not intervened to calm things down, he would have excommunicated the others.

We know the origin of the Quartodeciman custom. What needs to be explained is the origin of the other custom of breaking the paschal fast on the Sunday. Paschal homilies of the time show that both Quartodecimans and Sunday observers had the same idea of the Christian Easter as the feast of the salvation of the human race. So the difference was not theological, or at least was no longer so. In fact, it appears from remarks made by Irenaeus that the observance of Easter Sunday at Rome was of recent date, not earlier than Pope Soter (167–174). Furthermore, it is well known that Justin, who gives a very detailed picture of Christian life at Rome in his own time (around 150), never makes any kind of reference to Easter when he speaks of the Eucharist and the Lord's Day (*First Apology* 65-67). This evidence goes perfectly well with the fact that in the Synoptic Gospels Jesus gives no command to repeat the paschal rite during the Last Supper, and even announces the contrary, the interruption of Passover with himself. It seems, then, that the custom of observing Easter on the Sunday, defended by Victor, was a novelty, whereas the weekly Lord's Day was universally observed and is well attested in the

NT. For his part, Epiphanius, who came from Palestine and knew the country well, judged that Church controversies on the date of Easter only began in 135, after the disappearance of the Jewish-Christian bishops of Jerusalem (*Panarion* 70.9ff.), that is, after the disappearance of the group that kept alive the reference to the Jewish date of Passover.

After a Greek hierarchy with no custom of celebrating Easter had been installed at Caesarea, it is at least possible that those Nazoreans in Judea who joined forces with them after 135 exerted pressure to keep a tradition of paschal observance, which was then placed on the Sunday following Passover, so as not to give rise to any suspicion of Judaizing. However, if such a novelty was able to get established, travel as far as Rome, and maintain itself outside its original context, it must have had a natural *and traditional* meaning. The fact that the paschal celebration of the Quartodecimans, at least after 100, had the same structure as the weekly Saturday-Sunday vigil (see above, chap. 1, §II.2) could have facilitated such a transfer.

II. PENTECOST AND THE COVENANT

Despite being classed with the other two pilgrimage feasts, Pentecost does not appear to have as much substance to it as Passover and Tabernacles. In his vision of the future Temple, Ezekiel (45:17-20) foresees a complete ritual in which, however, Pentecost does not feature. Evidently it was not for him a feast with an eschatological dimension. According to the biblical data, it is dependent on Passover, as its name (Hebrew: "Weeks"; Greek: "Fifty [days]") implies; it lasts only one day and is not the occasion of special food laws. Finally, the gift of the Law at Sinai is not closely attached to Pentecost. According to Exodus 19:1, the Israelites arrived in the Wilderness of Sinai in the third month after leaving Egypt. Whatever the calculation used in relation to Passover, Pentecost does indeed fall in this month (Sivan), but that does not necessarily mean that this feast coincides with Moses' ascent of the mountain. In other words, the enormous importance of Pentecost in the Essene texts and in Acts 2 is an unexpected development.

The *Book of Jubilees* appears, as we have seen (chap. 2, §II.1), to have been known at Qumran. For this book, Pentecost, falling always on Sunday the fifteenth of the third month, is the greatest feast of the year. No particular link with Passover is mentioned. Despite its interest in questions concerning the calendar, *Jubilees* mentions no count of seven weeks. According to this book, Noah had already celebrated this feast of the Covenant with his sons. Then it was forgotten, but was partly restored with the patriarchs: the covenant made with Abraham between the divided animals, the birth of Isaac, and the covenant with Jacob all took place on this day. Later it was again forgotten by the Israelites, but the angel revealed it once more to Moses and ordered him to observe Pentecost in such a way that the Covenant would be renewed each year (*Jub* 6:10). The covenant sacrifice offered by Moses at Sinai (Exod 24:1-11) took place on the fifteenth of the third month.

In *Jubilees* 6:21 this feast has two names and is apparently twofold also in nature: feast of the First Fruits and feast of Oaths, or renewal of the Covenant. The two aspects are mutually complementary. The archetype is the deliverance from the Deluge: a new world begins after the chaos and disappearance of the old world; the sinners have been drowned; Noah and his sons represent the new humanity saved from the waters. This model is applied to the Israelites (5:17ff.): "If they are converted to God in justice, he will forgive all their transgressions and will pardon all their sins. It is written and decreed that he will show mercy to all those who are converted from all their faults once every year."

The ritual of the feast is not set out in detail, but it involves oaths, and there is a commentary (1:22ff.) in terms that recall Ezekiel 36:25-27: "They will not submit until they confess their own fault and those of their fathers. After that they will turn to me in all uprightness, with all their heart and all their soul [. . . .] I will create in them a holy Spirit and will purify them [. . .] and they shall all be called sons of the living God." The mention of the holy Spirit (instead of the new spirit of Ezekiel) is characteristic: it is the sign of belonging to the community and the Covenant by forsaking sin and by observance in conformity with the precepts.

In the *Damascus Document,* found in the famous Cairo Genizah and more recently at Qumran, the expression "new Covenant," which occurs in Jeremiah 31:31 with a purely eschatological meaning, turns up three times. In particular, the members of the community "have entered into a new Covenant in the land of Damascus" (CD 6:19; 8:21). The sinners are those who have "despised the Covenant and the pact they made in the land of Damascus." Strictly speaking, they are excommunicated. This Covenant is established by God with the "faithful remnant" (3:13). However, whereas Jeremiah 31:31 draws a contrast between an old covenant and a new one, there is no mention here of any "old Covenant." We should not forget that the Covenant made with Moses is only a renewal of that made with Noah and his sons and later forgotten. The "new Covenant" in the *Damascus Document* and at Qumran is therefore a return to the Law of Moses properly understood and observed, a refocusing on the Sinai event, but understood as a renewal of the forgotten Covenant, as there is never any question of a "covenant with Moses."

According to this outlook, the Covenant is not a mere juridical abstraction, not even the definition of a nation. This term also designates the community itself, inasmuch as it is faithful, for through it the Covenant exists concretely. This way of looking at the Covenant is not new; already in 1 Maccabees 1:15, "to separate oneself from the holy Covenant" was equivalent to leaving the solidarity of the community. The same meaning can be seen in Daniel 11:22ff., where the "head of the Covenant" is defeated, and then the Gentile king (Antiochus Epiphanes) fights against "the holy Covenant." In the Qumran *Community Rule,* to enter into the Covenant is no more and no less than to enter the community, as the rite of admission makes clear (1 QS 2:12, 18). Conversely, to enter the community is to be converted to the Law of Moses (5:7ff.). In consequence, Jews who are outside the community or members who have been excluded are outside the Covenant and are therefore as impure as the Gentiles.

It is easy to see that these questions are close to an entire body of Christian themes present throughout the NT, turning on the claim, which can properly be called sectarian, to be the true Israel. The prologue of the *Community Rule*, defining the community's project, says explicitly that it is a question of fixing norms for all Israel "at the end" (1 QS 1:1-5). Many commentators have already made comparisons with the NT.

Before developing two particular aspects in the following section, we shall simply emphasize two points already discussed from another angle. The typology of Noah for expressing the renewal of the Covenant leads directly to a very simple meaning given by Paul to the water of baptism: entry into the kingdom begins with a sign of passage through death; but now the sinners are not drowned but are delivered from their sin, which is transferred to Jesus Christ. Further, since the community of the Covenant has the monopoly of inspired interpretation of the Law of Moses, it can only reject, or at best ignore, other communities with parallel claims, unless some particular pressure forces a confrontation. This gives a context for the reciprocal (and relatively late) fulminations to be found in the Gospels and in the rabbinic sources, which we associated with the reorganization of Yavneh but which do not appear in properly Pauline Christianity.

III. ADMISSION AND EXCLUSION

Pentecost, when the Covenant is renewed, is also the day for receiving new members, whose admission into the community is thereby an entry into the Covenant. That is the general setting of the Pentecost of Acts 2, and it is also a cornerstone in the Essene customs (1 QS 5:8; *Jub* 6:17ff.). This likeness is hardly surprising, since we are dealing with circles that were originally alike. The procedure for admitting candidates throws light on the community's nature and structure, but it is fairly complex, and the information that we possess is scattered. For this reason we will follow the description of the Essenes given by Josephus (*J.W.* 2 §§119-160). It is full of details and fits in reasonably well with the documents from the Judean wilderness, but, above all, it is the only synthesis written for outside readers, whether Jewish or not, whereas the Qumran and similar texts are internal literature, and we do not know what authority they possessed.

1. INITIATION IN THE NAME OF THE TRINITY

Josephus implies that the process of initiation lasted three years (*J.W.* 2 §§137ff.). During the first year, in which the candidate remained outside the community, he was given a hatchet, a linen "girdle," and a white garment, and led the same kind of life as the Essenes. The hatchet was used for digging toilet trenches (2 §148). The linen girdle, which was much more than a simple loincloth, was "used" for the ablutions, then for the meals, and was regarded as sacred (2 §129); it was in reality a priestly vestment, the *abnet* of Exodus 28:39, analogous to the veil hiding the Holy of Holies (Exod 26:31). The white garment was the normal garb of the Essenes, probably symbolizing purity. So the sacred ritual of the meal, which was prepared by priests (see below) had a sacerdotal and cultic dimension.

With all these elements the candidates were being trained in the Essene way of life, including purifications, while remaining outside the community; in other words, they took their meals apart, presumably with their fellow novices. If, at the time determined, they had given proof of self-mastery, they were allowed to come closer to the Essene life by sharing in the "purer waters" of purification. They were not yet admitted to the common exercises, in particular the meals, which were taken in a place regarded as a sacred shrine where no profane person might penetrate. So there was a gradation in the purifications.

This second phase lasted two years, and if the candidates had given proof of character, they were admitted into the community; but before taking part in the meals, they had to pronounce "fearful oaths." Before discussing them, we recall that these phases are very much like those in the Qumran *Community Rule* (1 QS 6:13-23), although the latter does not mention garments and has a rather different way of presenting access to the "purity," that is, the community meal. We recall also that the stages of admission to the *ḥaberim* fraternities involved the reception of certain garments (chap. 5, §V.1).

Basically, there is a central element common to all these groups, which is the community meal. The groups of neophytes lead the same life as the community proper, but are separated according to several stages of access to the meal, which is therefore the element that defines the community and gives its identity. It is significant that this was precisely the reproach made to Peter after his visit to Cornelius ("You have eaten with them"—Acts 11:3) and that the decrees of James, according to their original meaning, had among other effects that of avoiding unwanted contacts and, implicitly, the sharing of meals (cf. above, chap. 5, §I.1).

The oaths, according to Josephus, are eleven, and "it is by oaths such as these that the Essenes bind the new members" (2 §142), which may imply that the list is not fixed, or more probably, that he is making a selection. In first place is a commitment to "venerate the divinity, and to observe justice to men." This is precisely the goal of John the Baptist's preaching, according to Josephus (*Ant.* 18 §116) and is not far removed from the twin commandments recalled by Jesus in Mark 12:29 par.: love of God (Deut 6:5) and love of the neighbor as oneself (Lev 19:18). This global commitment obviously covers everything but needs to be made more specific by further oaths.

Certain rules of the group do not form part of the list of oaths but can be classed with them, either because of their importance or because of the penalty attached. Thus Josephus states that they "have the greatest reverence, after God, for the name of the lawgiver; whoever blasphemes it is punished by death" (2 §145). Josephus also mentions, as a common norm, the general prohibition of pronouncing the name of God, a blasphemy punishable by stoning. Blasphemy is really a deviation of the oath or benediction; it is only to be expected in the case of God, but less so in that of Moses, for what could an oath sworn by Moses be? Similarly, CD 15:1-5 forbids swearing by God, even under a roundabout form, and by the Law of Moses. Decoded, this means that the only lawful oaths are the "fearful oaths" of the new members, and they are pronounced in the name of God and *in the name of Moses*. If to that is added the fact that entry into the Covenant is nothing else than the reception of the Holy Spirit, who presides over the actualization of the Law of Moses, it can immediately be seen that entry into the community, marked by a final purification, is placed under a very simple threefold sign: God, Moses, and the Spirit. We are not far from Matthew 28:19, where the risen Lord commands the Eleven to baptize "in the name of the Father and of

the Son and of the Holy Spirit"; all that has happened is the sub-
stitution of Jesus for Moses. The greater novelty is conveyed by
the first half of the same verse: "make disciples of *all nations*."

2. TABLE FELLOWSHIP AND PENALTIES

The oaths are fearful because they involve responsibility, so
there are penalties attached to them. Josephus says only that those
who are caught in or convicted of serious faults are expelled from
the community but that they remain bound by their oaths and so,
not being able to touch profane food, they die of starvation (*J.W.* 2
§143). Expulsion is therefore principally a removal from the community meal. Josephus's brevity is somewhat disappointing, but it
has the merit of focusing attention on what is essential. The precepts and oaths taken all together converge on food, and in particular on the community meal, which has a sacred structure:
according to *Ant.* 18 §22, *priests* prepare the bread and other
food. Although there is no mention of meat, these meals resemble
communion sacrifices, eaten in the sanctuary, which fills out what
has been said concerning the holiness of the garment and of the
place: the community itself is the sanctuary.

The Qumran documents give many details, but they do not
depart from this pattern: the penalties imposed can be defined in
terms of a greater or lesser degree of removal from the "purity," the
community meal. CD 9:16-23 distinguishes two areas: serious
wrongs against God or the neighbor, and crimes involving money.
For a serious fault to be judged and punished, there have to be
three witnesses, corresponding perhaps to three successive occasions. When a breach of the law has occurred, the witness must
make a deposition before an officer of the court in the presence of
the accused. Once two testimonies have been recorded independently, whether relating to the same wrongdoing or to two successive occasions of the same nature, the one accused is excluded
from the "purity" as a precautionary measure, since his guilt has
not yet been legally established. In accusations concerning property, two testimonies are enough to prove the charge, but even after
only one, the accused is removed from the "purity" as a similar
precautionary measure. In fact, Deuteronomy 19:15 requires "two

or three witnesses to sustain any charge," which leaves some room for interpretation.

Penal procedure is somewhat better defined in CD 9:2-8, which introduces an essential element—the warning. No one may accuse another without proving that he has already warned him personally; otherwise the accuser is guilty of either carrying out a vendetta or even of being an accomplice. The result is that the first offense generally carries no consequences, except private warning or remonstrance. Thus in 2 Corinthians 13:1, Paul cites Deuteronomy 19:15, indicating that he is now on the third warning, that is, this is the third time that the same faults have occurred; at his next visit he will have the right to punish any further backsliding. He is not talking of a criminal trial or sentence but of excommunication. There too, the number of witnesses is understood as the "number of testimonies."

The same is true in Matthew 18:16, where two or three warnings have to be given before the judgment of the community and finally exclusion. To be regarded as a Gentile or a (Jewish) tax collector represents maximal impurity, in which Gentiles and Jews who do not belong to the community are lumped together. The impurity thus acquired, which has precise juridical consequences, symbolizes the reality of sin. It is an echo in reverse of the pedagogy of entry into the community, in which the various purifications are the outward signs of an inward distancing from sin, but without any magical effect, as Josephus emphasizes with regard to John the Baptist (*Ant.* 18 §117).

There are clear analogies here with the Christian practice of excommunication, whether permanent or temporary, the latter being the basis of the Church's penitential system.

IV. WHY *CHRISTIANI?*

Jesus and his disciples were from the beginning called "Nazoreans," a term that has been kept in Syriac and Hebrew. Again, as we have seen, the Latin term *christiani,* given by the Romans to messianic agitators, was pinned on the disciples at Antioch at a time of disturbance. This name has stuck in Greek and in Latin. That it should have done so is all the more remarkable in that

Pauline Christianity is not strictly speaking a messianism: "Christ" has become a proper name, and the Pentecost narrative of Acts 2 is careful to sidestep the final (messianic) question of the disciples, who await the establishment of the kingship of Israel (Acts 1:6). We may well wonder why NT Christianity, especially with the new horizons opened up by Paul, still felt the need to retain a polemical link with Judaism by declaring itself the "New Covenant" and transforming messianism instead of cutting all such ties and launching out into entirely new waters.

If the names of Christ (Anointed) and Christian have been preserved, even though turned aside from their primitive meaning, it can only be because they originally had an appreciable significance, presumably connected with an anointing. Moreover, in a culture as sensitive to signs as Judaism, we need to start by looking, not for clever juggling of verses or subtle biblical allusions to a king-Messiah or a priest-Messiah, but to concrete points of reference, that is, following the method we have used until now, rites rather than events or doctrines.

Let us say it at once: the available information is too tenuous to come to certain conclusions. We shall have to be content with presumptions based on convergent indications and distinguishing two parts: first concerning anointings properly so called, then some observations on the sign of the cross.

1. CHRISTIANS, ANOINTINGS

The NT never speaks of ritual anointing except of the sick (Mark 6:13; Jas 5:14). Laying on of hands is often mentioned, but in circumstances so diverse that it is difficult to draw specific implications, apart from the quite banal fact that it is an official gesture. The major fact that obliges us to study the NT more closely is the later testimony of the Christian canonico-liturgical tradition. The *Apostolic Tradition,* attributed to Hippolytus of Rome, at the beginning of the third century, but showing all the signs of strict conservatism, describes the admission of a neophyte. After being baptized (no definite minister is indicated), the candidate receives from a presbyter an anointing with oil, then is confirmed by the bishop, who pours oil on the head, lays a hand on the head, and makes a sign on the forehead. Having then received the Spirit, the new member enters into the people and is allowed to receive the kiss of peace, which is the first gesture of the Eucharist proper (*Apostolic Tradition* 22:3).

Of course, the mere fact of writing down a ritual in such minute detail implies that there were controversies or at least divergent traditions. The Syriac tradition attests another sequence: anointing with oil by the bishop, then baptism, and finally imposition of an outward mark (the cross), which closes the rite. This arrangement is fairly parallel to the narrative of the man born blind (John 9:6ff.) and has analogies with the accounts in Acts 9 and 10 of the baptisms of Saul and Cornelius. These variants do not, however, obscure the presence of two distinct blocks: a baptism without any specialized minister, which is none other than the conclusion of a catechumenal process, and a body of admission rites performed by the bishop or under his responsibility and consisting of one or more anointings and the imposition of a sign.

Were these gestures created by the Church, or do they go back to the first generation? In other words, are they of Jewish origin? In a general way, the series of rituals described by Hippolytus has clear Jewish counterparts. The remarkable exception is precisely the body of rites of confirmation by the bishop. The ancient Jewish sources provide no clear positive attestation. There is, however, an interesting piece of indirect evidence. Deuteronomy 6:8 prescribes the wearing of phylacteries on the arm and "between the eyes," which seems to indicate the forehead. However, the Mishnah (*MMen* 4:8) declares that wearing the phylacteries on the forehead is "the usage of the *minim*" and that they should be worn on top of the head. The reasons given for this decision are a little artificial: we may well suspect that there is something on the forehead of the *minim* which for them attracts the phylacteries and for the rabbinic tradition repels them.

The phylacteries contain "all the words," that is, the essentials of the Torah. That being so, comparison with the rite of confirmation described above suggests a possible answer: if someone has received an anointing with oil and the sign of the cross on the forehead, putting the phylactery on the same spot is equivalent to saying that the Torah rests on symbols that are typically Christian, or at least have become so. If the comparison can be justified, it would mean that both the anointing and the sign of the cross were of Jewish origin, at least among Essenes and *ḥaberim.*

So we need to push the investigation further, looking in the NT for tiny indications, even if we do not expect to find clear mention of these things because of concern not to publish the rites.

In Luke 4:18, Jesus applies to himself the verse of Isaiah 61:1: "The Spirit of YHWH is on me, by which he has anointed me, to proclaim a good news." In Acts 10:37ff., Peter tells how Jesus, after the baptism that John proclaimed, had been anointed by God with spirit and power. A similar expression already occurs in Acts 4:26 (Jesus anointed by God), with a quotation from Psalm 2:1-2, in which the kings of the earth fight against YHWH and against his anointed. The reference is royal, not sacerdotal, and allows a comparison with Pilate's notice, in which Jesus is described as king of the Jews (John 19:19). However, Jesus' own declaration, quoting Isaiah, has rather a prophetic reference. All these expressions, which certainly indicate an authority and a mission, do not, however, correspond to any clearly identifiable gesture.

In the NT there are some curious images associated with the Spirit. According to Mark 1:8 and John 1:33, John the Baptist proclaims that the one who is to come will baptize in the holy Spirit (Matthew 3:11 and Luke 3:16 add "fire"). Even if "baptize" simply means to plunge, without any technical specification, this expression makes an odd combination of the idea of immersion (in water) and the Spirit. In any case, there is another way of expressing the gift of the Spirit that is biblical but equally strange. It is given by Paul in Titus 3:6: "God has poured out this Spirit on you through Jesus Christ." Similarly, Peter in his speech at Pentecost (Acts 2:17) quotes Joel 3:1 ("I will pour my spirit on all flesh").

These two formulations express two quite distinct ways of representing the gift of the Spirit, but in the last analysis neither evokes the breath of the Spirit (see John 3:8; 20:22) or the Spirit's sudden irruption (Acts 19:6), both striking metaphors evoked by the literal meaning of the Hebrew and Greek words translated as "spirit," that is, "wind." On the contrary, both formulations suggest in the background a concrete gesture that is applicable not directly to the Spirit but to something that symbolizes the Spirit, whether by "plunging in" or "pouring out." In the first case the reference would be baptism, or at least a certain stage in the baptismal course; in the second one might think of Ezekiel 36:25f. "I will pour out over you a pure water . . . ; I will put my Spirit in you."

In any case, "plunging" and "pouring" are not the same as "anointing" (see Exod 29:7). In particular, the question remains: In what sense can Jesus and his followers be described as "anointed"? Let us here recall the astonishing scene known as the "anointing at Bethany." A woman pours a precious perfume on the head of Jesus, who declares to his astonished disciples that she has prepared his body for burial and that wherever the gospel is proclaimed, what she has done will be told in memory of her (Matt 26:13; Mark 14:9). This narrative, coming just before the Last Supper and forming a kind of diptych with it, has therefore enormous importance. What does it mean? By embalming, especially with a highly scented perfume, a corpse escapes corruption and stench, with the symbolic meaning of escaping death. By her gesture, then, the woman foretells the resurrection, or more exactly Jesus interprets it this way, just as he interprets the bread and wine of the Last Supper. But if we look at the gesture itself, Jesus, who until then has refused any kingship, accepts, as if taken by surprise, something that resembles a royal anointing.

But that is not all. In 2 Corinthians 2:14-16, Paul says: "Through us, God spreads in every place the perfume of his knowledge. In fact, we are for God the good odor of Christ (of the Anointed) for those who are being saved and for those who are being lost; for some, an odor of death leading to death, for others an odor of life leading to life." Paul generally is not very imaginative, and the metaphor used here is certainly not without some basis in reality. It presupposes a gesture of anointing, with a sweet-smelling substance, both "us" and Jesus. Here we find a further dimension of the gesture performed by the woman at Bethany, which explains its permanent significance: like Jesus, the disciples present and future receive a fragrant anointing that signifies their death and their resurrection.

Other passages also suppose an anointing received by the disciples. John declares to his correspondents: "You have an anointing from the Holy One" (1 John 2:20). Paul develops a similar idea in 2 Corinthians 1:21: "It is God who gives us the anointing, who has marked us with his seal." In this last statement, in which Paul, as is his wont, attributes to God the existence and life of the communities, it is difficult not to suppose that he is guided by a concrete gesture.

In the end, however, we have to admit that all these texts hardly convey more than a rumor of anointing, probably with a diversity of customs. All the same, one fact emerges: despite the imprecision of the narratives, there is somewhere a mark symbolizing the Spirit that is distinct from the water of baptism. In John 3:5 Nicodemus is invited to a twofold rebirth, from water and the Spirit. In Galatians 3:23ff., three phases can be perceived: justification by faith is linked up with baptism; then it is followed by the sending of the Spirit (4:6), and finally by the cross. Hebrews 5:13 makes a distinction between the milk of beginners and the solid food of the "perfect," that is, those who have finished with the initiation, who have received the laying on of hands after the baptisms (6:2). Even in Acts 19:3, where Paul appears to say that baptism in the name of Jesus gives the Spirit, the sequel shows that "baptism in the name of Jesus" is followed by the laying on of hand(s) followed by the irruption of the Spirit.

All these allusions are made in passing, without bothering about a description, and the terminology used is imprecise. Still, they probably allow us to affirm that the tradition reported by Hippolytus has Jewish roots. But we have not yet reached firm ground, either concerning the rites themselves or concerning a link with the Covenant and Pentecost. In order to try to get a little more precision, we need now to examine the "sign" with which the forehead of the candidate is marked, namely, the cross.

2. THE SIGN OF THE CROSS

We have already come across various allusions to the cross as a sign. The most remarkable is the shape of the paschal lamb, roasted on two spits in the form of a cross. The most symbolic case is confirmation by the bishop, who anoints the forehead with oil and marks a cross as a seal. However, it appears difficult to find an intrinsic link between these two. It is possible to take a roundabout way by interpreting the whole of baptism "in the name of Jesus" as the transfer of a debt, which was a regular use of the expression "in the name of XY." The result is for the baptized the annulment of his or her debt, which is the content of Jesus' inaugural proclamation of the year of forgiveness (Luke 4:19). In strictly banking terms, a certificate of debt was annulled by drawing two lines across it in the form of a cross, apparently a fairly natural gesture. In this way the mark of a cross on the forehead, traced with the thumb, can easily represent the forgiveness of sins, that is, redemption through the cross of the slaughtered lamb. The conjunction is even more natural if it can be shown that the cross on the forehead *preexisted* any strictly Christian significance. If an anointing with oil (made with the finger) is added, it becomes possible to identify the two essential elements in the oddly matched expression "a crucified Messiah," with reference either to Jesus or to his followers ("if we die with him"). That does not, however, imply that they had this meaning at the beginning.

There is in fact a biblical model. In Ezekiel 9:1ff., a man clothed in linen (an angel) stands in the midst of the destroyers who are going to chastise Jerusalem, and YHWH says to him: "Go through the city, through Jerusalem, make a mark on the forehead of all those who groan and lament because of the abominations which are committed within her." The word for "mark," translated "sign" by the LXX, is the last letter of the Hebrew alphabet, *thaw.* This mark on the forehead is very similar to that of the blood of the paschal lamb put on the lintels of doors (Exod 12:7) and perhaps also put as a "memorial between the eyes" (Exod 13:9, 16), so also on the forehead. The same passage of Ezekiel, translated independently of the LXX, is in the background of Revelation 7:3ff., where the angel who arises from the east holds God's seal but may not destroy anything until the elect (the 144,000) have been marked on the forehead by this seal; the same is enjoined on the angel with the fifth trumpet (Rev 9:4). An analogous idea can be perceived in Ephesians 4:30, "Do not grieve the Holy Spirit, in whom God has conferred on you a seal in view of the day of your deliverance." The constant element in these metaphors is an official seal (on the forehead). They appear to be based on more than a simple literary borrowing, as the term used (seal) is stronger than that in Ezekiel. In the same spirit CD 9:10-12 declares, quoting the prophecy of Ezekiel, that when the Anointed of Aaron and Israel (that is, the two Messiahs, Priest and King) arrive, those who are marked with the *thaw* on their forehead will be saved.

Tertullian affirms that this *thaw* was precisely the sign of the cross (*Against Marcion* 3.22). This was no personal invention. About the same time, Origen cites the opinion of a Jew, "one of those who believe in Christ": the shape of the *thaw* in the ancient Hebrew writing resembles the cross and prefigures the future sign on the forehead of Christians (*Selecta in Ezechielem,* PG 13.800d).

This information given by the Jewish-Christian on the shape of the *thaw* is exact and can even be filled out. In the ancient Hebrew alphabet, which is no longer in use, two letters have more or less the form of a cross, that is, of a simple mark: the first, *aleph,* and the last, *thaw,* both liable to alternate between the signs + and X. Now, in Revelation 1:8 we read: "I am the *alpha* and the *omega,* says the Lord God." Here the first and last letters of the Greek alphabet express that God is the beginning and the end of all things; but in the context the declaration applies equally well to Jesus Christ, "who has freed us from sin by his blood" (Rev 21:6).

If we transpose the terms of this statement from the Greek alphabet to the ancient Hebrew alphabet, it becomes: "I am the *aleph* and the *thaw,*" that is, "I am the + and the X." Earlier in Revelation we read that no one can open the book except "a lamb standing as if slain" (5:6). It is possible to infer that the cross of the paschal lamb is superimposed on the first and last letters of the alphabet: the crucified Jesus provides the key to the alphabet and ultimately to Scripture itself. Thus, through a sort of symbolic pun, the cross fulfills Scripture: "All is accomplished," is precisely what Jesus says on the cross (John 19:30). All this symbolism is linked to Hebrew. In Greek, however, it is even simpler, especially if there is also an anointing with oil. In the Greek alphabet the sign X is the letter *chi,* the initial of the verb to "anoint" and of the title *Christos.* This is the most direct way of understanding Revelation 22:4: "And his name shall be written on their forehead."

The clarity of this symbolism of the cross should not, however, obscure the fact that it brings together two series of elements that are quite distinct. One is the instrument of Jesus' death, with three unequal branches, to which is attached the preparation of the paschal lamb. The other is a mark (on the forehead) in the form of a cross, upright or on its side, with four equal branches and several different meanings, direct or annexed (cancellation, seal, alphabet). That these two realities should come together in a common symbolism presupposes that both preexisted independently. That is obvious for the first. As for the second, the rabbinic tradition, whose basis is close to the marginal customs of the *ḥaberim,* never takes any interest in other religions for their own sake, following in this a very biblical custom. In other words, the very energy with which that tradition objects to placing a phylactery on the forehead betrays that it was familiar with another sign on the forehead, which had now become associated with the *minim.*

3. CONCLUSIONS

The simplest conclusion to all these observations would be that Hippolytus's description of the bishop's reception of a new member, by anointing with oil and marking the forehead with a cross, is only a Christian reinterpretation of a gesture coming unchanged from Jewish fraternities of Covenant renewal, whether zealot or not. The cross, as a simple mark with a number of possible meanings, was originally an official gesture of affiliation made by the "overseer." It would then be easy to see how some of these "anointed ones," proclaiming the end and the imminent arrival of "the Anointed One" (the Messiah), could have been called by the Roman authorities *christiani,* that is, partisans of "Christus" or "Chrestus" understood as a proper name.

It would be equally easy to take hold of certain aspects of Paul's religious culture as, in all likelihood, an "anointed" messianist. The parallel between the seal of the Spirit at baptism (Eph 1:13) and the seal of circumcision (Rom 4:11) suggests a rite. When he declares that he has not been sent to baptize but to evangelize, "not in the wisdom of rhetoric, so that the cross of Christ will not be voided" (1 Cor 1:17), Paul is not necessarily expressing lack of interest in signs in themselves but rather his sense of a mission to give them another, "fuller" meaning. That is to say, the cross (a simple mark) on the forehead of one anointed already existed as a customary sign concluding the baptismal course; by preaching it was given the new meaning of "the cross of Christ," combining death and life (resurrection, new creation). This brought about a complete mutation of messianism, which ceased to be centered on Jerusalem and could be carried "even to the ends of the earth" (Acts 1:8).

Chapter Seven

And Jesus?

At the end of our investigation of the origins of Christianity, we need to ask: Who, or rather what, was Jesus? The elements of an answer to this question have already been given in the course of this book, but it may be useful to bring them together. The purpose is not to compose a biography of Jesus but to suggest what his contemporaries might have thought of him.

The simplest synthesis is expressed by the two disappointed disciples who were walking to Emmaus after the crucifixion of Jesus (Luke 24:13ff.). Whatever may be the literary nature of this narrative, what they have to say about Jesus certainly reflects the ideas and expectations of many. In response to the question of the Stranger, who seems not to know about recent events in Jerusalem, they reply:

> What happened to Jesus the Nazarene, who had shown himself a prophet powerful in deeds and in words before God and before all the people; how our chief priests and our leaders gave him up to be condemned to death and crucified him. As for us, we were hoping that he was the one who would deliver Israel; not only that, it is two days since these things happened. But some women of our company gave us a shock. They went very early in the morning to the tomb, and when they didn't find his body, they came back saying they had had a vision of angels who said that he is living. Some of us went to the tomb and found things as the women had said; but they didn't see him (Luke 24:19-24).

Now this portrait of Jesus accords in essentials with that given in a highly interesting text known as the "Slavonic (Old Russian)

Version" of the *Jewish War* of Flavius Josephus (hereafter SJ). There it is one of a number of passages (no.12; see the Appendix, p. 174f.) that do not correspond to anything in the standard text of the *Jewish War*. These "additional passages" deal, for the most part, with the history of Judea and Josephus's own campaigns, and it is very difficult to see why they would have been introduced into the text by someone else, for instance, a Christian interpolator. Instead, when the SJ is compared with the standard text, it looks, by and large, like the sort of thing which Josephus himself tells us he wrote for the benefit of Jews and others living in the Parthian kingdom and which he subsequently revised, with the help of assistants, to produce the *Jewish War* as we have it (see *J.W.* 1 §§1-6).

Some few of the "additions," such as no. 12, do, it is true, have a Christian interest. But they cannot be easily dismissed as forgeries. First, they are written in the same style as the others that have no Christian interest. Second, they express, as do the disciples on the road to Emmaus, an entirely Jewish view of Jesus. Third, a number of important details in these passages disagree with the biography of Jesus given in the Gospels. On the last two scores we might have expected a Christian forger to give himself away. The passage concerning Jesus is given as an appendix. We shall quote it from time to time in our present discussion.

1. "A PROPHET POWERFUL IN WORDS AND IN DEEDS"

For Jesus' contemporaries, he was a or even *the* "Nazorean." For the meaning of this term, we refer the reader back to chapter 5, §II.2; suffice it to recall here that it was equivalent to "Son of David." That he was a teacher and a healer is abundantly clear from the Synoptic Gospels. But he was, according to them, more than that. He was, to use the words of the disciples on the way to Emmaus, "powerful in words." The meaning of that expression is illustrated by the reaction of the crowds to Jesus' teaching in Matthew 7:28-29: "(they) were deeply struck by his teaching, for he was teaching them as one having authority and not as their scribes." The authority displayed by Jesus was not his own; it came from the fact that, unlike the scribes, who could only repeat the Torah, Jesus had the power of the Spirit to make the Scriptures speak today. In that sense Stephen, too, was "powerful in words" and Apollos "powerful in the Scriptures" (see Acts 6:10; 18:25).

The power of God with Jesus was also manifested in deeds, especially of healing. This aspect is especially emphasized by the SJ, where Jesus is not named but is referred to throughout as "the Wonderworker." This text does not mention explicitly his teachings, but his "power in words" is brought to the fore: "And everything whatsoever he wrought through an invisible power he wrought *by word and command.*" Similarly, in Acts the apostles and others are "powerful in deeds" (see 4:30; 5:12; 6:8). Both the Gospels and the SJ mention accusations that, in healing, Jesus broke the Sabbath. To this charge the SJ provides a subtle and characteristically Jewish defense that is not found in the NT and would hardly have occurred to a Christian interpolator: Jesus did not heal with his hands but by simple word of mouth, so he did not break the Sabbath by "working."

Such evidence of divine power provoked the question of what kind of being this might be. The Gospels provide an echo of such debates: "Some say John the Baptist, others Elijah, others Jeremiah or one of the prophets" (Matt 16:14 par.). Similarly, according to the SJ, "Some said of him, 'Our first lawgiver (Moses) is risen from the dead and hath performed many healings and arts,' while others thought he was sent from God." Note how these speculations suppose the belief that some great person of the past might return from the dead endowed with superhuman powers. Indeed, the opening sentences of SJ no. 12 even wonder whether Jesus was really human or something more than human. Perhaps it was to counter notions that Jesus was not truly human that Paul, writing to the Galatians, emphasizes, somewhat oddly, that he was "born of a woman" (Gal 4:4). In any case, such speculations do not appear to go beyond what was thinkable to first-century Jews. We know that they imagined that the Messiah would be both human and superhuman, perhaps preexistent, perhaps even in some sense divine.

The disciples on the way to Emmaus call Jesus a "prophet," the term used by those who marvel when he brings back to life the son of the widow of Nain: "A great prophet has arisen among us, and God has visited his people" (Luke 7:16). This miracle recalled those of the OT prophets Elijah and Elisha (see 1 Kgs 17:17-24; 2 Kgs 4:32-37).

2. "WE WERE HOPING . . ."

The second part of the crowd's exclamation at Nain expresses the conviction that Jesus was the one through whom God had promised to "visit" his people—in other words, that he was "the one who would deliver Israel." We have seen in the course of this book the nature of such expectations. That they were affirmed of Jesus is the evidence of both the Gospels and of the SJ no. 12: "and many souls were in commotion, thinking that thereby the Jewish tribes might free themselves from Roman hands." The agent of this deliverance was, of course, the Messiah (though the term is not used either by the disciples on the way to Emmaus or by the SJ). The point to be made immediately is that the identity of the Messiah was not known in advance; it would be known for sure only when he had accomplished his task. In the meantime, signs might be observed that would indicate who he would be.

Jesus was not the only one around this time who was thought by some to be the promised deliverer. Two, who arose in the forties and fifties of the first century A.D., are mentioned both by Josephus and the Acts of the Apostles. One was the Theudas named by Gamaliel in Acts 5:36. According to Josephus (*Ant.* 20 §§97-98), he persuaded the masses to take their belongings and follow him to the Jordan River, which he said would part at his command; this was evidently to be a reenactment of the entry into the Promised Land. The Roman governor Cuspius Fadus sent a squadron of cavalry against him. Theudas and many of his followers were killed, and others were taken prisoner.

Another who was considered the promised deliverer was the unnamed "Egyptian" for whom Paul is taken in Acts 21:38. Josephus writes of him both in the *War* (2 §§261-263) and in the *Antiquities* (20 §§169-172). He gathered his followers on the Mount of Olives, from where he proposed to force an entrance into Jerusalem, overpower the Roman garrison, and set himself up as "tyrant" (that is, king). According to the version in the *Antiquities,* he promised that the walls would fall at his command. Governor

Felix killed, captured, or dispersed his followers, but he himself escaped.

In the Gospels Jesus repeatedly refuses to be recognized as Messiah. A decisive episode is recorded in John 6:14ff., where, after Jesus has fed the multitude in the wilderness around the time of Passover, people said: "He really is the one, the prophet who is to come into the world." Then, we are told, Jesus realized that they were going to come and take him away to make him king, so he fled once more into the mountains all alone. Similarly, the SJ records that those who saw the deeds of the "Wonderworker" (Jesus) invited him to lead them in the liberation of Jerusalem: "Now when they saw his power, that he accomplished whatsoever he would by (a) word . . . they . . . made known to him their will, that he should enter the city and cut down the Roman troops and Pilate and rule over us . . . ." It is not clear in the SJ whether he accepted this invitation; the text is doubtful. One manuscript continues, "but he heeded not," whereas others have "he disdained not."

In all four Gospels Jesus makes a public entry into Jerusalem, during which he is acclaimed as the King-Messiah. It was, by all accounts, a peaceable and orderly event, perhaps meant to be a symbolic gesture. As a "triumphal entry," it could have been judged a failure. It may well have sent mixed signals to observers, both friendly and hostile: Did he intend to oust the Roman occupiers or not?

3. "OUR LEADERS GAVE HIM UP"

The Jewish authorities in Jerusalem had every reason, from their point of view, to be alarmed at the rise of messianic fervor around Jesus. It was only too likely to draw down Roman repression and retribution. Their predicament, and the obvious solution to it, are recounted in an episode in John's Gospel (11:47ff.); whether or not it is strictly historical, this narrative reflects the political realities of the situation. The leaders met together in council and asked: "What are we to do? This man accomplishes many signs. If we let him do them, everyone will believe in him, and the Romans will come and destroy our Holy Place and our nation." It is the high priest Caiaphas who replies: "You understand nothing. Do you not see that it is better for one man to die than for the entire nation to perish?" They subsequently handed Jesus over to Pilate.

In the SJ, when knowledge came to the Jewish leaders that Jesus had been urged to take Jerusalem and reign as king, they assembled together with the high priest and reflected: "We are powerless and (too) weak to withstand the Romans. Seeing, moreover, that the bow is bent, we will go and communicate to Pilate what we have heard, and we shall be clear of trouble, lest he hear (it) from others and we be robbed of our substance and ourselves slaughtered and our children scattered." And they went and told Pilate.

Jesus was crucified. According to John 19:19, the charge sheet over his cross read: "Jesus the Nazorean, the king of the Jews." He was a "king who never reigned," as another passage of the SJ puts it (no. 20).

Jesus' death naturally put an end to the hopes that had been entertained that he was the promised liberator. Now we can understand why the two disappointed disciples of Luke 24 were making their way to Emmaus. Most commentators on this aspect of the episode have given their attention to identifying the spot, in terms of its reported distance from Jerusalem. More interesting for us is its significance. For Emmaus was the place where, in 164 B.C., Judas Maccabeus won the decisive battle that opened the way to Jerusalem and resulted in the capture and purification of the Temple (1 Macc 4:1ff.). So, after losing hope in Jesus, these disciples go, or return, to a place hallowed by a successful armed struggle against the Gentile oppressor. Their journey symbolizes the rise of militant activism recorded by Josephus in the decades that preceded the disastrous revolt in 66.

4. ". . . WHO SAID THAT HE IS LIVING"

Rumors that Jesus was risen from the dead, but also denials of the fact, are reported in the SJ, addition no. 21 (see the Appendix, p. 175f.). Jews in the first century held different views about life after death. For those who, like the Pharisees, believed in resurrection, it was not perhaps beyond the bounds of possibility that for an exceptionally righteous person, God might, as it were, anticipate the general resurrection. That, at least, seems to be admitted by the Pharisees to whom Paul appeals in Acts 23:6ff. We have also noted that according to both the Gospels and the SJ, people surmised that Jesus might be a prophet from the past risen from the grave.

According to Acts 3–4, Peter and those around him experienced the power, here and now, of Jesus' name in the cure of the disabled man at the Beautiful Gate of the Temple. They used it as an argument against the Sadducees, who denied resurrection. Similarly, the power of the Holy Spirit, the Spirit of Jesus, at work among them was proof that he had been raised from the dead and exalted to God's "right hand," from where he had sent the Spirit on his followers (Acts 2:14-35). The empty tomb and apparitions were no longer ambiguous but supported and gave shape to their conviction that Jesus lives.

So Jesus was after all the Messiah and would now or very soon proceed to carry out the Messiah's task of national liberation. This renewed messianic hope is expressed by the question put to the risen Jesus by his disciples in Acts 1:6: "Lord, is it at this time that you are going to restore the kingship in Israel?" His ascension to heaven signifies a delay; at the same time, there is an assurance that at some future time, known only to God, Jesus will return to carry out the task (see Peter in Acts 3:20ff. and Paul in 1 Thess 4:13ff.).

That was not, however, the final position of NT Christianity. Luke, in the conclusion of the episode that we have been following in this chapter, relates that the risen Jesus, arrived at Emmaus, took bread, blessed God, broke the bread, and gave it to the two disciples, and they recognized him *in the breaking of the bread.* The sacramental action signifies the transformation both of messianic hope and faith in the resurrection of Jesus. He is already here, and the kingdom of God has arrived.

Conclusion

Christianity came from an environment whose religious culture was close to that of the Essenes. In that environment new members were admitted into the community through a process of initiation featuring special ablutions. The central action of the community, which was strictly reserved to the initiates, was a sacred meal in which bread and wine were taken in symbolic portions. These central features are still familiar to Christians under the names of baptism and the Eucharist. The rites themselves are inherited from the original environment; what is new in Christianity is the meaning that they convey through the saving death and resurrection of Christ. Around them were clustered other characteristic structural elements of community life and order that can be traced both in the original environment and later in the Christian Church.

The religious culture of the original environment was marginal to the rest of contemporary Judaism and of a markedly sectarian type. It can be called broadly "Essene," an umbrella term meaning "Faithful," which in fact covered a number of groups and subgroups. Those who belonged to this movement saw themselves as constituting the true Israel, alone keeping the Covenant and charged with preparing the way for the Lord who would soon come to judge the world. Other folk, both Jewish and Gentile, were regarded as wicked and impure. Many such groups looked out for the Messiah; some anticipated his appearance by militant activism. In such an environment any sort of opening to the Gentiles was unthinkable. It cannot be explained by the nature of the particular Galilean environment from which Jesus' first disciples came. That was highly traditional and looked toward Babylonia as well as toward Jerusalem.

That Gentiles would turn to the God of Israel, especially in the last times, had been foretold by some of the prophets. What could not have been foreseen was the inclusion of Gentiles along with Jews to form one communion. That was truly an upheaval, threatening a return to chaos if it were not perceived as a new creation. It was seen by its proponents as an effect of the resurrection of Jesus and of the gift of the Spirit, both events that overturned boundaries.

The characteristic episodes in the story, as well as the position of the principal actors, can be summed up in the following table. The three main vertical columns are defined by three fundamental ways of looking at Jesus: as disciple of John the Baptist (which can be further subdivided), as Messiah, and as Lord. To take the case of Paul, he first identified the Messiah (Christ) as Jesus, then Jesus Christ as Lord, inaugurating a kingdom without boundaries, as expressed in Philippians 2:11: "That every tongue proclaim that Jesus Christ is Lord."

Horizontally, there are three phases. One is static, tied to the memory of Jesus and earlier than Pentecost (or what Pentecost stands for). In the second, in a climate of agitation about the right "way," Jesus is identified as the Messiah who is about to return. The third is characterized by the Spirit, and messianism, strictly so called, has disappeared, or rather has been transformed: the Messiah has already arrived (resurrection), and "Christ" becomes a special proper name or a sort of surname. For the chief persons, a Roman numeral indicates the principal stages in their evolution.

This table is complex, but it is an extreme simplification of a great number of small facts that have never fallen into any ready-made scheme. Three points stand out. First, James, brother but not disciple of Jesus, becomes the reference point after the dispersion following the disappearance of the Master. Next, the enormous convulsion caused by messianizing agitation, under Caligula and afterward, led to contacts with Gentiles, brought about by popular movements, which broke down the barriers isolating the God-fearers. Finally, Peter ends up in a position mid-

	Jesus (John's baptism)			Messiah	Lord
	Nazorean	Teacher	Healer	(about to come)	(already come)
Phase I (Jesus)	James (brothers of Jesus)	Apollos	Peter I, Barnabas	Paul I, Aquila	
Phase II ("Way")		joins Aquila (Corinth)	*(christiani)*	Paul II (Damascus, Antioch)	
Phase III (Spirit)	James (Nazoreans, Jerusalem)		Peter II (resurrection, Cornelius)		Paul III (Ephesus; neither Jews nor Greeks)

way between that represented by James, who does not change (passive expectation within the original circle) and Paul (long-term movement toward the nations). Of the three, Peter alone is properly speaking a disciple of Jesus. Like James, he stays close to the original environment. Like Paul, but rather differently, he has, under the influence of the Spirit, an active sense of Jesus' resurrection as already effective here and now.

For Further Reading

Readers who wish to have further information or documentation concerning the views expressed in this book should refer to Étienne Nodet and Justin Taylor, *The Origins of Christianity: An Exploration,* A Michael Glazier Book (Collegeville, Minn.: The Liturgical Press, 1998).

The following is in no sense a bibliography of Christian origins but simply a short list of important studies of major topics dealt with in the present work.

Bradshaw, Paul F. *The Search for the Origins of Christian Worship.* London: Society for Promoting Christian Knowledge, 1992.

Collins, John J. *The Scepter and the Star: The Messiahs of the Dead Sea Scrolls and Other Ancient Literature.* The Anchor Bible Reference Library. New York: Doubleday, 1995.

Freyne, Seán. *Galilee from Alexandria to Hadrian: A Study of Second Temple Judaism.* Wilmington, Del.: Michael Glazier, 1980.

Hengel, Martin. *The Zealots: Investigations into the Jewish Freedom Movement in the Period from Herod I until 70 A.D.* Trans. David Smith from the 2nd German edition, 1976. Edinburgh: T. & T. Clark, 1989.

Horbury, William. *Jewish Messianism and the Cult of Christ.* London: Student Christian Movement Press, 1998.

Metzger, Bruce. *The Canon of the New Testament: Its Origin, Development, and Significance.* Oxford: Clarendon Press, 1987. Reprinted with corrections, 1988.

Murphy-O'Connor, Jerome. *Paul: A Critical Life.* Oxford: Clarendon Press, 1996.

Nodet, Étienne. *A Search for the Origins of Judaism: From Joshua to the Mishnah.* Journal for the Study of the Old Testament, Supplement

Series no. 248. Trans. Ed Crowley from the French edition, 1992. Sheffield: Sheffield Academic Press, 1997.

Schürer, Emil. *The History of the Jewish People in the Age of Jesus Christ (175 B.C.–A.D. 135).* A New English Version Revised and Edited by Geza Vermes, Fergus Millar, and Martin Goodman. 3 vols. Edinburgh: T. & T. Clark, 1973–1987.

Stemberger, Günter. *Introduction to the Talmud and Midrash.* Translated from the 2nd German edition, 1992, and edited by Markus Bockmuehl. 2nd ed. Edinburgh: T. & T. Clark, 1996.

Thackeray, H. St. John. *Josephus: The Man and the Historian.* First published in 1929 as the Hilda Stich Stroock Lectures at the Jewish Institute of Religion; new edition with an introduction by Samuel Sandmel. New York: Ktav Publishing House, 1967.

VanderKam, James C. *The Dead Sea Scrolls Today.* London–Grand Rapids, Mich.: Society for Promoting Christian Knowledge–Wm. B. Eerdmans, 1994.

The "Slavonic" Josephus

The following passages are translated by H. St. J. Thackeray from a German rendering of the "Slavonic" (Old Russian) version of the *Jewish War.* They can be found, among a total of twenty-two "principal additional passages in the Slavonic version" in an appendix to volume 3 of the Loeb Classical Library edition of the works of Josephus, where they are completed by a table of "omissions in the Slavonic version." Here they are reproduced without the square brackets introduced by Thackeray to indicate what he considered to be Christian interpolations.

(12) The Ministry, Trial and Crucifixion of "The Wonder-worker" (Jesus) [Between *J.W.* 2 §§174 and 175]

At that time there appeared a man, if it were permissible to call him a man. His nature and form were human, but his appearance (was something) more than (that) of a man; notwithstanding his works were divine. He worked miracles wonderful and mighty. Therefore it is impossible for me to call him a man; but again, if I look at the nature which he shared with all, I will not call him an angel. And everything whatsoever he wrought through an invisible power, he wrought by word and command. Some said of him, "Our first lawgiver is risen from the dead and hath performed many healings and arts," while others thought that he was sent from God. Howbeit in many things he disobeyed the Law and kept not the Sabbath according to (our) fathers' customs. Yet, on the other hand, he did nothing shameful; nor (did he do anything) with aid of hands, but by word alone did he provide everything.

And many of the multitude followed after him and hearkened to his teaching; and many souls were in commotion, thinking that thereby the Jewish tribes might free themselves from Roman hands. Now it was his custom to sojourn over against the city upon the Mount of Olives; and there, too, he bestowed his healings upon the people.

And there assembled unto him of ministers one hundred and fifty, and a multitude of the people. Now when they saw his power, and that he accomplished whatsoever he would by (a) word, and when they had made known to him their will, that he should enter into the city and cut down the Roman troops and Pilate and rule over us, (*text doubtful, either* he disdained us not, *or* but he heeded not).

And when thereafter knowledge of it came to the Jewish leaders, they assembled together with the high-priest and spake: "We are powerless and (too) weak to withstand the Romans. Seeing, moreover, that the bow is bent, we will go and communicate to Pilate what we have heard, and we shall be clear of trouble, lest he hear (it) from others, and we be robbed of our substance and ourselves slaughtered and our children scattered." And they went and communicated (it) to Pilate. And he sent and had many of the multitude slain. And he had that Wonder-worker brought up, and after instituting an inquiry concerning him, he pronounced judgment: "He is a benefactor, not a malefactor, not a rebel, nor covetous of kingship." And he let him go; for he had healed his dying wife.

And he went to his wonted place and did his wonted works. And when more people assembled round him, he glorified himself through his actions more than all. The teachers of the Law were overcome with envy, and gave thirty talents to Pilate, in order that he should put him to death. And he took (it) and gave them liberty to execute their will themselves. And they laid hands on him and crucified him (*text doubtful, either* contrary to the law of their fathers, *or* according to the law of the emperors).

(21) The Rent Veil of the Temple and the Resurrection [After *J.W.* 5 §214]

This curtain was before this generation entire, because the people were pious; but now it was grievous to see, for it was suddenly rent from the top to the bottom, when they through bribery delivered to death the benefactor of men and him who from his actions was no man.

And of many other fearful signs might one tell, which happened then. And it is said that he, after being killed and after being laid in the grave, was not found. Some indeed profess that he had risen, others that he was stolen away by his friends. But for my part I know not which speak more correctly. For one that is dead cannot rise of himself, though he may do so with the prayer of another righteous man, unless he be an angel or another of the heavenly powers, or (unless) God himself appears as a man and falls and lies down and rises again, as pleases his will. But others said that it is not possible to steal him away, because they set watchmen around his tomb, thirty Romans and a thousand Jews.

Glossary of Terms and Names

AQIBA: a rabbi who supported Simon Bar Kokhba in the second Jewish revolt; he specialized in the attachment of oral traditions to Scripture.

BAR KOKHBA, SIMON: the military leader of the second Jewish revolt against Rome (A.D. 132–135).

CANON: a Greek word meaning "rule"; the official list of recognized books of the Old or New Testament.

DIATESSARON: the harmony of the four Gospels made by Tatian about A.D. 170, arranged so as to form one continuous narrative.

ETHNOS: a Greek word meaning "nation"; here, of the Jews in the Hellenistic period (after 300 B.C.).

EXILE, THE: of inhabitants of Judah deported to Babylon after the capture of Jerusalem by Nebuchadnezzar in 587/586 B.C.; in 538 the Persian king Cyrus permitted those who wanted, to return to Jerusalem.

GAMALIEL: the name of two important rabbis of the first century A.D.: Gamaliel I, in the early part of the century, was the teacher of the future apostle Paul, according to Acts 22:3; his grandson Gamaliel II, toward the end of the century, played a leading part in the formation of rabbinic Judaism.

GOD-FEARER: a Gentile sympathetic toward Judaism.

ḤABER (PL: ḤABERIM): a Hebrew word meaning "companion"; here, a member of a *ḥabura*.

ḤABURA: a fraternity, entry into which required a process of initiation and whose members took part in common meals eaten in conditions of strict ritual purity.

HASMONEAN(S): the royal dynasty (so named after an ancestor) founded by the Maccabees, which ruled over an independent Jewish state until Judea came under Roman rule after 63 B.C.

HEROD: in the NT three different rulers are called Herod: (1) Herod the Great, who became king of Judea under Roman supervision in 37 B.C. and died in 4 B.C. (see Matt 2:1); (2) his son Herod Antipas, who ruled Galilee and Perea with the title of "tetrarch" from 4 B.C. to A.D. 39 (see Luke 1:5); (3) Herod Agrippa I, grandson of Herod the Great and king of Judea from A.D. 41 to 44 (see Acts 12:1).

HILLEL: flourished in the last quarter of the first century B.C., regarded as one of the founders of the rabbinic tradition.

JOSEPHUS, FLAVIUS: Jewish military leader in Galilee during the first revolt (A.D. 66–70), who turned himself over to Rome and became the Roman historian of the Jews.

KERYGMA: a Greek word meaning "proclamation"; here, that of the saving death and resurrection of Jesus Christ.

MACCABEES, THE: Judas Maccabeus ("the Hammer"), Jonathan, and Simon, sons of the priest Mattathias, who led a successful revolt of the Jews against King Antiochus IV after 166 B.C.

MASSORETIC TEXT (frequently abbreviated as MT): the Hebrew text of the Old Testament definitively established by the Massoretes, Jewish scholars active between A.D. 750 and 1000.

MINIM: a Hebrew word meaning "sectarians"; rabbinic sources after A.D. 70 use this term to designate, among others, Jewish disciples of Jesus.

MISHNAH: a Hebrew word meaning "repetition"; the codification of the Jewish oral Torah made around A.D. 220.

NAZOREAN (or NAZARENE): probably from a Hebrew word meaning both a "shoot" (*neṣer* see Isa 11:1) and "to observe" *naṣar;* it is an epithet given in the NT and elsewhere both to Jesus (and his "brothers") and to his followers.

PENTATEUCH: the first five books of the Bible ("Books of Moses"): Genesis, Exodus, Leviticus, Numbers, Deuteronomy.

PHILO: a Jewish writer at Alexandria in the first half of the first century A.D., who explained his religion to his Greek and Roman contemporaries.

PRE-CONSTANTINIAN: the period of the history of the Church before the reign of Constantine the Great (A.D. 285–337), who began the process by which Christianity became the official religion of the Roman Empire.

SEPTUAGINT (frequently abbreviated as LXX): the Greek translation of the Old Testament begun at Alexandria from about 250 B.C.

SYNOPTIC: from a Greek word meaning "seen together"; the three Gospels of Matthew, Mark, and Luke have many passages in common; they can be compared by placing them side by side in a "synopsis."

TANNAITES: from a Hebrew word meaning "repeater"; the earliest handers-on of the rabbinic tradition until the compilation of the Mishnah.

TORAH: a Hebrew word meaning "instruction," frequently translated as "law"; the written Torah is the Pentateuch, and the oral Torah is the tradition; according to the rabbis, both were received by Moses at Sinai.

TYPOLOGY: the interpretation of persons or things in the OT as "types," that is, prefigurations, of persons or things in the NT; for instance, King David was a "type" of Christ.

YAVNEH (also called JAMNIA): a town near Jaffa that was the home of a rabbinical school founded after the first revolt in A.D. 70.

YOḤANAN BEN ZAKKAI: the founder of the school at Yavneh.

Index of Scriptural References

(listed in the order given in the Jerusalem Bible)

Genesis

1:2	27
1:3	31
8:20	122
9:4ff.	122
9:22	122
15:7ff.	51

Exodus

12:1ff.	47, 50, 143, 144
12:6	44
12:7	158
12:9	142
12:22ff.	51
12:25	68
12:26ff.	47
12:43ff.	84
13:9	158
13:16	158
19:1	145
23:17	51
24:1-11	146
24:8	51
26:31	149
28:39	149
29:7	156

Leviticus

15:1-18	28
16:6ff.	39
17:1ff.	120
18:5ff.	122
19:18	150
23:11	32

Numbers

19:14-15	29
19:18ff.	84

Deuteronomy

6:4ff.	24
6:5	150
8:10	48
16:1ff.	68
19:15	151, 152

Joshua

5:10ff.	50

1 Kings

17:17-24	165

2 Kings

4:32-37	165
5:14	36

Judith

12:7	36

Esther

3:12ff.	68

1 Maccabees

1:15	147
2:42	73
4:1ff.	167
5:14ff.	59

Psalms

2:1-2	155
40:7 LXX	15

Sirach (Ecclesiasticus)

34:25	36
54:25	53

Isaiah

6:9-10	137
8:23	57
11:1-16	53
11:1	127
11:10	135
40:3	102
53:1-12	15
53:11	37
61:1	155

Jeremiah

31:31	51, 147

Ezekiel

9:1ff.	158

33:2-9	107
36:25-27	146, 156
45:17-20	145

Daniel

11:22ff.	147

Joel

3:1	155

Amos

9:11ff.	120

Malachi

3:1ff.	37

Matthew

2:23	125, 126
3:2	35, 38
3:3	103
3:8	38
3:11	155
3:13-15	37
3:15	42
4:8ff.	71
4:15	57
4:17	35
7:28-29	163
8:8	27
10:5-6	2
11:2-6	37, 41
11:16-19	35
11:21	70
12:46-50	140
13:55	125
14:13-34	70
15:32-39	70
16:14	164
16:19	25

16:22	72
17:1ff.	136
18:16	29, 152
18:18	25
23:15	87, 90
26:13	156
26:21	48
26:26-29	49f.
26:26	46
26:29	50, 51
26:69	125
26:71	125
28:12-15	136
28:16-20	59, 136
28:19	2, 42, 150
28:20	110

Mark

1:4	38
1:5	38, 42
1:8	155
2:1	70
2:18-20	40
3:20	70
6:13	153
6:14	35
6:29	41
6:30-44	54
7:1ff.	71
8:28	35
9:11-13	35
9:33	70
10:38-39	36
11:27-33	35
12:29	150
14:9	156
14:18	48
14:22-25	49f.
14:22	46
14:25	50

Luke

1:68	122
1:78	32
2:32	137
3:8	38
3:16	155
3:18	38
3:21	36
4:16-30	137
4:18	155
4:19	158
6:2ff.	138
7:16	164
7:18-23	41
7:33	39
11:1-4	35
11:1	41
11:38	71
12:50	36
18:37	126
22:1ff.	138
22:15-20	49
22:15-18	50
22:17-19	47
24:13-35	162
24:13	167
24:35	33, 55

John

1:29	38, 48
1:33	155
1:37	41
1:45-51	135
2:6ff.	43
2:13ff.	43
3:5	43, 157
3:8	155
3:22–4:2	43
3:22-24	35
3:22	28

3:23	36, 110
3:25	43
3:26-30	41
4:10	43
4:21-23	73
4:35-38	136
6:1	70
6:14-15	166
6:26-59	48
7:27	135
7:41-42	135
9:6ff.	154
9:22	135
11:47-53	166
11:50	93
12:19-23	136
12:42	135
13:1ff.	44
16:2	135
18:5	126
18:7	126
19:19	126, 155, 167
19:25-27	140
19:30	159
20:21-23	136
20:22	155
21:1ff.	139

Acts of the Apostles

1:6	71, 153, 168
1:8	22, 161
1:14	140
1:22	55
2:1-41	51, 141, 145, 148, 153
2:13-14	27
2:14-35	168
2:17	155
2:22	126
2:37ff.	41
2:38	9, 35, 40

2:41	109, 114
3:1ff.	168
3:6	126
3:7	114
3:15-16	9
3:15	114
3:20-21	168
3:20	128
4:4	114
4:10	114, 126
4:13	72
4:26	155
4:30	164
4:31	27, 114
5:12	164
5:13	114
5:17	126
5:33-34	138
5:35-39	41, 73, 93
5:36	165
6:8-10	104
6:8	164
6:10	164
6:14	126
7:48	114
8:1-40	26
8:1	115
9:2	102, 112
9:17-19	154
9:18	113
9:20-22	113
9:20	103
9:23ff.	113
9:26-27	112
9:26	113
9:31	113
9:36-42	30
10:1–11:18	2, 26
10:1-2	27
10:37-43	155
10:44-48	154

10:47	40	23:6	138, 168
11:3	120	24:5	126
11:19-26	98f.	24:14	102
11:20	26	24:22	102
11:26	97	26:9	126
13:15	90	28:26-29	137
13:42-44	137	28:28	26
13:45	137		

Romans

13:46	26, 107	4:11	160
13:50	137	6:3-11	9
15:1ff.	138	6:3-4	42
15:5	27, 82, 126	11:11-12	137
15:12-22	119f.	13:11ff.	32
15:19	99		

1 Corinthians

15:21	22	1:2ff.	106
16:8-11	29	1:12	105
17:16-34	89	1:17	160
18:1-3	94, 103	3:6	109
18:4-7	106	4:15	105
18:6	26	5:7-8	48
18:7	89	11:23-26	45, 49f.
18:8	104	11:24	54
18:18-21	107	11:26	32, 55
18:24-26	102	15:20	32
18:25	37, 164	16:12	105
18:27-28	104		

2 Corinthians

19:1-7	41, 108f.	1:21	157
19:3	37, 157	2:14-16	156
19:6	40, 155	11:32	112, 113
19:8-10	111	13:1	152
19:9	102		

Galatians

19:11-12	116	1:12-17	112
19:23	102	1:15-16	114
20:6-12	29, 30	1:17	113
20:8	31	1:18-19	115
20:16	37, 115	1:18	112
21:38	165	1:21	113
22:3	95, 138		
22:4	102, 112		
22:8	126		
23:1-10	138		

2:1ff.	138
2:9	100, 121, 138
2:11-14	119, 121
3:23ff.	157
4:4	164
4:6	157
6:15	85

Ephesians

1:13	160
4:30	158

Philippians

2:9	118
2:11	170
3:6	95

1 Thessalonians

4:13ff.	168

Titus

3:6	155

Hebrews

5:1ff.	39
5:13	157
6:2	157
10:5	15

James

5:14	153

1 John

2:20	156

Revelation (Apocalypse)

1:8	159
5:5	135
5:6	159
7:3ff.	158
9:4	158
22:4	159
22:16	135

Index of Non-Scriptural References

I. CHRISTIAN SOURCES

Clement of Rome

Corinthians
13:2   14

Didache
9:4   54

Epiphanius of Salamis

Panarion
29   125
70.9ff.   145

Eusebius of Caesarea

Eccles. History
3.20.1-6   125
3.27   128, 132
3.35   128
3.39.1-7   15
4.5.2-4   124, 128
5.23-24   144

Hippolytus of Rome

Apostolic Tradition
22.3   154

Ignatius of Antioch

Ephesians
18   41

Philadelphians
8   14

Irenaeus of Lyons

Against the Heresies
1.27.2   16
3.1.1   139

Demonstration
99   16

Justin Martyr

Dialogue
40.3   142
80.4   36

First Apology
31.6   129
65-67   144
67.3   15

Melito of Sardis

fr. 9   142

Paschal Sermon   144

Origen

In Ezechielem   159

Tertullian

Against Marcion
3.22   159

Prescription
36   139

II. JEWISH SOURCES

Flavius Josephus

Jewish Antiquities
1 §3   22
1 §16   23
1 §§22f.   22
3 §318   23, 89
14 §§172ff.   66
14 §§220ff.   91
14 §§421ff.   62
15 §§3-4   66
15 §370   66
17 §§23ff.   62
17 §§41ff.   64
17 §289   63
18 §§4f.   63
18 §22   151
18 §23   92
18 §§37ff.   79
18 §84   89, 93
18 §116   150
18 §117   38, 152
18 §118   90
18 §§261ff.   98
20 §§34ff.   82
20 §§49-53   89
20 §§97-98   165
20 §§139ff.   82
20 §§169-172   165

Jewish War
1 §§1-6   163
2 §§119-160   148
2 §119   85
2 §128   31
2 §129   149
2 §§137ff.   81, 149
2 §141   20
2 §142   53, 150
2 §143   151
2 §145   150
2 §148   31, 149
2 §150   85
2 §§174f.   174
2 §§261-263   165
2 §§430ff.   74
4 §130   76
4 §137   36
4 §444   76
5 §214   175
7 §45   89, 97
7 §§407ff.   92

Life
20ff.   74

Jubilees
1:22ff.   146
5:17ff.   146
6:10   146
6:17   51, 148
6:21   146
14:1ff.   51
29:7   51

Philo of Alexandria
Contempl. Life
64-90   31

Legation
185ff.   98
200-203   76

Qumran Texts

CD (Damascus Document)
2:11-12	51
3:13	147
6:19	147
8:21	147
9:2-8	152
9:10-12	159
9:16-23	83, 151
15:1-5	150

1 QM
9:8f.	29

1 QS
1:1-5	148
2:12	147
2:18	147
2:25-3:12	39
3:4	51
3:6-9	39
5:7ff.	147
5:8	19, 39, 148
5:13	39
5:20	19, 39
6:4-5	52
6:13-23	81, 149
6:15	19, 39
6:21f.	83
8:1-16	19
8:12ff.	103
9:3-10:8	19
9:12f.	19

1 QSa
2:11-22	52

1 QSb
3:26	53
5:20ff.	53

4 QFl
1:11-13	53

4 QMMT   52

4 QPB
3-4	53

11 QT
18-22	52
43	52

Rabbinic Texts

BBabaB
60b	82

BKer
9a	85

BMeg
13a	76

BBer
28b	77

BShab
31a	84

BYeb
46b	83
47a-b	82

Canticle Rabbah
2:16	78

MAb
1:1	20
1:10ff.	64
1:16	77

MBer
8:5	31

MHag
2:7	80

MMen
4:8	154

MOhol
18:7   29

MPes
7:1   142
7:2   143
8:8   84

MSanh
1:1   83

TAbZ
8:4   121

TDem
2:2ff.   80

TNida
9:14   28

TOhol
1:4   28

YPes
6:1 p. 33a   64

YShab
16:8, p. 15d   76

YShebi
9:1, p. 38d   79

III. OTHER ANCIENT
    SOURCES

Corpus Papyr. Judaicarum

II, n° 153   96

Suetonius

Claudius
25   94

Nero
16   95

Tacitus

Annals
15.44   96